Vegan Athlete Cookbook

**101 Flavorful Plant-Based Recipes
For Health, Strength, and Athletic Performance**

Copyright © 2013 by Zoey Sampson

All rights reserved. This book or any portion thereof may not be reproduced or used in any manner whatsoever without the express written permission of the publisher except for the use of brief quotations in a book review.

Printed in the United States of America.

First Printing, 2013

TABLE OF CONTENTS

SPORTS DRINKS & SMOOTHIES

Mango Shake with a Coconut Twist 8

Choconut Butter Shake 9

Blueberry and Vanilla Smoothie 10

Strawberry and Chocolate Smoothie 11

Tutty Fruity Shake 12

Fresh Pear and Ginger Whizz 13

Rooibos Tea and Blueberry Smoothie 14

Lemon and Lime Tang 15

Mango Citrus Tingle 16

Taste of the Tropics 17

Green Kiwi Fruit Smooth 18

ENERGY BARS & FOOD ON THE RUN

Vanilla and Almond Bars 20

Nutty Chocolate Protein Bar 21

Pecan Nut Munchies 22

Cinnamon and Corn Cookies 23

Dried Fruit and Coconut Chews 24

Blueberry Flax Granola 26

Strawberry Energy Bar 28

Crunchy Granola Bars 29

Chocolate Coconut Quinoa Slices 31

Apple and Nut Chews 33

Banana Carob Bars with a Chili Twist 35

Energy Bars the Vegan Way 36

NOODLES, QUINOA AND RICE

Raw Pad Thai 39

Herbed Quinoa and Hemp 40

Bean Ball Spaghetti 41

Mushroom Spirals 43

Macaroni and Vegetables 45

Garlicky Bean Pasta 47

Quinoa and Braised Mixed Vegetables 48

PIZZA PERFECT

Bean and Tomato Pizza 51

Vegetable Pizza on a Beet and Sunflower Seed Crust 53

Adzuki Bean Pizza 55

TOFU AND TEMPEH

- Sloppy Joes 58
- Tofu with Sugar Snap Peas 59
- Tempeh with a Nutty Sauce 61
- Tempeh with Black Bean Sauce 63
- Curried Tofu 65
- Korean Tofu Salad 67
- Sweet Potato Curry with Caramelized Shallots 69

BEANS, PEAS AND LENTILS

- Lentils and Veggies with a Zip 72
- Red Lentils with an Indian Flavor 73
- Pistachios and Beans 74
- Nutty Bean Croquettes 75
- Coconut Rice with Black Beans 76
- Corn and Black Bean Patties 78
- Almonds and Beans 80
- Pumpkin Seeds and Garbanzo Beans 81
- Indian Beans and Rice 82
- Piccata Nut and Chickpea Medallions 84

Crispy Chickpea Rissoles 86

South Sea Island Beans and Rice 88

Tuscan Rapini Beans 90

Aduki Beans and Greens 91

Barbequed Black-Eyed Pea Rolls 93

Pinto and Plantain Stew 94

SOUPS

Ginger Soup 97

Carrot and Ginger Soup 98

Butternut Apple Soup 99

Hot and Sour Mushroom Soup 100

Summer Curry Soup 102

Corn Chowder 103

Thai Lemongrass Soup 105

Chili Lentil Soup with Pineapple 107

BURGERS & NOT-MEAT MEALS

Almond and Flaxseed Burgers 110

Veggie Burgers 111

Vegan Bacon 113

Bean and Beet Burgers 115

Portabello Mushroom Burgers.. 117

Broccoli 'Beef' with Quinoa 119

WRAPS & SANDWICHES

Eggplant and Hoisin Open Sandwiches 122

Grilled Onion and Eggplant Bread Rolls 124

Saucy Wheatball Subs.. 125

Celeriac Wraps.. 127

SALADS, VEGGIES & SIDES

Celery and Beetroot Salad 129

Fresh Kale and Cranberry Salad 131

Chili Corn Salad with Beans and Tomatoes 132

Couscous Salad with Dried Fruits and Edamame...................... 133

Cranberry and Nut Salad.. 134

Curried Cucumber and Mango Salad....................................... 135

Cabbage and Nectarine Chinese Salad 136

Summer Squash and Pasta Salad 137

Zucchini Pasta Salad 139

Cauliflower Salad 140

Summer Salad with Poppy Seed Dressing 141

Summer Fruits with Chickpeas 142

Stuffed Acorn Squash 143

Curried Sweet Potatoes 144

SAUCES & DIPS

Tahini-Miso Sauce 147

Barbeque Sauce 148

Baba Ghanoush 149

Creamy Spinach and Artichoke Dip 150

Sweet Chili Sauce 151

POWER PACKED PUDDINGS & COOKIES

Chocolate Zucchini Cupcakes 153

Cookies a la Vegan! 155

Fruity Chocolate Chip Scones 156

Corn and Chia Waffles 158

Pineapple Upside Down Cake 159

Date and Blueberry Muffins 161

Cranberry and Lemon Cookies 163

No Bake Oat Cookies 165

101 Flavorful Plant-Based Recipes For Athletic Performance

FOREWORD

Hello there my fellow beautiful Vegan!

My name is Zoey. I love cooking all things Vegan, and of course, as per the nature of this recipe book, it's important to mention here that I also love keeping active.

Mentioning athleticism in the same discussion as talking about adhering to a strict Vegan diet is oft times met with a raised eyebrow and a look of disbelief. To many, not educated in the matter, the two don't seem to go hand in hand.

Bro-science body builders who swear by an unwavering animal heavy source of protein are fairly stalwart in their beliefs as to what constitutes performance foods for weight gain through lifting and cardiovascular exercise.

Regardless of the mode of training, it's uncommon to see a lot of literature even outside of these circles touting the pros of a Vegan athletic lifestyle.

Yet, it's apparent to everyone that meets me, that as a happy and wholesome Vegan, I'm doing just fine, eating above my caloric baseline when trying to gain muscle and size, and below when cutting.

I'm proud of my endurance and endless energy, and in fact, as I sit down to write this, I'm not long back from my morning 3 mile run.

And guess what? I'm not sitting here dying from lack of energy or nutrients. In fact... I feel fantastic!

Vegan Athlete Cookbook

In reality, the myths surrounding a Vegan diet causing low energy levels, and inability to perform or grow have absolutely no scientific backing to support them.

It's simply a matter of making sure your macros are in order.

Plant based foods have allowed me to have a bounce in my step and a healthy outlook on life for years.

In fact, many successful sportsmen and women in the world are Vegans, including Triathletes, Cyclists, Bodybuilders, Mixed Martial Artists, Wrestlers, Rock Climbers and yes, there are even Olympians amongst us.

Sure, I became a Vegan for the fairly obvious reason to avoid animal cruelty (don't get me started – this is not the time Zoey!), and soon after, I noticed how well I was feeling. Nothing had suffered, and only benefits were to be found.

In fact, I wasn't just doing well, I honestly felt damn fantastic. Not eating meat or dairy was doing wonders for how I felt about what I was putting into my body, and although I admit I was surprised at first, my training was still right on track.

Let's talk more about the protein... Here's a question we are always sick of hearing from many a meat eater. Where are the building blocks for muscle? Where is the protein? Can this be found in a Vegan diet?

Well where do I start? Veggies such as spinach, soy milk, nut butter, quinoa, lentils, chickpeas, tofu, peanut butter, almonds... The list goes on – and variety is the buzz word.

101 Flavorful Plant-Based Recipes For Athletic Performance

Healthy fats? Yes, these are a preferred energy alternative to high GI carbs to get the calories up there when we are lifting and trying to pack on the muscle! And of course a great quality source of fats can be found in avocados, olives and raw nuts!

Vitamins, like bone strengthening calcium are in abundance in all dark green vegetables, soy products and orange juice, all Vegan friendly of course.

It's not rocket science. Protein, and fats aren't exclusive to the butcher.

You know what? I have a feeling I'm preaching to the converted.

We know this stuff. We don't need convincing.

So after discovering a lack of easy to find Vegan recipes that support a performance focused lifestyle, and myself being such a devotee to the art of the kitchen creation, this little recipe book was born.

Fancy a Green Kiwi Fruit Smoothie? Or some Pecan Nut Munchies to put in your backpack? Or how about winding down with a Vege Pizza? Yummo!

Energy bars? These are a delicious boost. I cannot lie.

The key to my power packed diet is variety. Fruits, vegetables, plenty of leafy greens, whole grain products, nuts, seeds, and legumes are only a part of what gives me my incredible energy.

You'll enjoy making many of the dozens of main meals - the pizzas, soups tofu and sandwiches, salads and more, all brimming with energy, and containing a nice balance of healthy fats,

Vegan Athlete Cookbook

proteins, low GI carbs, bursting with plant sterols and spices, perfect for kicking goals and for feeding our fitness fanaticism!

How about a sweet yet healthy snack? After you've finished with this book, you should have plenty in the fridge!

Here is 101 amazing tasting recipes to showcase our life changing diet, to keep us pounding the pavement, busting out those extra reps in the gym, and keep you looking and feeling awesome!

From here on the path to personal power through Vegan scrumptious goodness is yours to command.

Peace, and enjoy the journey!

Zoey

101 Flavorful Plant-Based Recipes For Athletic Performance

DISCLAIMER

Before we get started, a quick note on the nutritional information found at the bottom of each recipe.

Simply put, I've done my best to fastidiously calculate the macro nutrient breakdown, however obviously there will be variations in everyone's exact kitchen creation depending on several factors, brand choices etc.

So please, understand that as a general rule they should be fairly close in the calculations, and are included primarily to serve as a beneficial guide to keeping you on track.

I certainly hope that the info proves useful and accurate to your needs and goals, and of course if you wish to double check my calculations on any recipe, I would always recommend that you please do so if you feel the need.

Vegan Athlete Cookbook

SPORTS DRINKS & SMOOTHIES

101 Flavorful Plant-Based Recipes For Athletic Performance

MANGO SHAKE WITH A COCONUT TWIST

Mangoes and Coconut – classic flavor but up to date taste! Quite delicious and absolutely moreish! For a thicker shake substitute one of the cans of coconut milk with coconut cream.

Serves 2

INGREDIENTS:

3 ounces vanilla rice protein

4 cups frozen chopped mangoes

2 (14 ounce) can low calorie Coconut Milk

2½ cups icy water

DIRECTIONS:

1. Place all of the ingredients into a blender or smoothie maker.
2. Whizz up for about 30 seconds until nice a smooth consistency.
3. Serve in a tall glass.

Nutritional Facts per Serving: *Calories 747, Fat 25.0g, Carbs 74.1g, Dietary Fiber 10.1g, Protein 36.6g*

Vegan Athlete Cookbook

CHOCONUT BUTTER SHAKE

The classic combination of chocolate and peanuts gives this health drink a very satisfying flavor. Enjoy this shake anytime. It also makes a wonderful dessert!

Serves 2

INGREDIENTS:

4 ounces chocolate rice protein

4 tablespoons peanut butter

16 ounces low calorie chocolate almond milk

2 cups crushed ice

DIRECTIONS:

1. Place all of the ingredients into a blender or processor.
2. Whizz up for about 45 seconds until you have a nice blended mixture.
3. Make sure that the peanut butter has been well mixed in.
4. Serve with a sprig of mint on the top.

Nutritional Facts per Serving: *Calories 442, Fat 22.1g, Carbs 21.6g, Dietary Fiber 8.3g, Protein 52.2g*

101 Flavorful Plant-Based Recipes For Athletic Performance

BLUEBERRY AND VANILLA SMOOTHIE

This one could not be easier! Make sure you have plenty of blueberries in the freezer or switch it up with raspberries if you would prefer.

Serves 2

INGREDIENTS:

4 ounces vanilla rice protein

4 cups frozen blueberries

1 pint of chilled water

DIRECTIONS:

1. Place all of the ingredients into a blender or smoothie maker.
2. Whizz up for about 30 seconds until nice a smooth.
3. Serve in a tall glass.

Nutritional Facts per Serving: *Calories 392, Fat 1.0g, Carbs 49.6g, Dietary Fiber 10.7g, Protein 47.5g*

Vegan Athlete Cookbook

STRAWBERRY AND CHOCOLATE SMOOTHIE

A taste of summer all year round if you fancy it! The classic taste of chocolate and strawberries! What a pleasure!

Serves 2

INGREDIENTS:

4 ounces of chocolate rice protein

4 cups frozen strawberries

2 tablespoons Omega oil blend

1 pint iced water

DIRECTIONS:

1. Place all of the ingredients into a blender or processor
2. Blend for 30 seconds or more so as to produce a smooth mixture.
3. Serve

Nutritional Facts per Serving: *Calories 442, Fat 16.7g, Carbs 39.5g, Dietary Fiber 11.4g, Protein 43.2g*

101 Flavorful Plant-Based Recipes For Athletic Performance

TUTTY FRUITY SHAKE

A perfect shake for instant energy and a feel good after effect! Experiment with different soft fruits. It is always good to use what is in season. Enjoy.

Serves 2

INGREDIENTS:

1 large fresh peach – pit removed

1 sliced mango

1 cup fresh or frozen strawberries

4 tablespoons vanilla protein powder

1 tablespoon coconut butter

1½ tablespoons coconut oil

1½ cups unsweetened apple juice

Sweetener to taste

A handful of ice cubes

DIRECTIONS:

1. Skin the peach and the mango.
2. Place all of the ingredients into a blender.
3. Blend together for about 45 seconds until the shake is of the desired consistency.
4. Add more sweetener if desired.
5. Serve with some chopped mango or peach on the top.

Nutritional Facts per Serving: *Calories 439, Fat 16.0g, Carbs 56.3g, Dietary Fiber 6.4g, Protein 23.0g*

FRESH PEAR AND GINGER WHIZZ

A wonderful mix of flavors to give you that 'get up and go' feeling! Use chocolate rice protein if you fancy a change of flavor.

Serves 2

INGREDIENTS:

1 large ripe banana

1 small ripe pear

2 cups icy water from the fridge

1 tablespoon ground flax seed

1 tablespoon vanilla rice protein

1 tablespoon freshly grated ginger root

DIRECTIONS:

1. Peel the banana.
2. Quarter and de-pip the pear
3. Place all of the ingredients into a processor or blender.
4. Add a few ice cubes if the mixture is not cold enough.
5. Serve in tall glasses.

Nutritional Facts per Serving: *Calories 150, Fat 1.4g, Carbs 27.8g, Dietary Fiber 5.8g, Protein 8.1g*

101 Flavorful Plant-Based Recipes For Athletic Performance

ROOIBOS TEA AND BLUEBERRY SMOOTHIE

Make that body sing with this fruity energy boost! Rooibos tea (also known as red bush tea) is an excellent source of antioxidants. Use it freely in your shakes and feel it doing you good.

Serves 2

INGREDIENTS:

1 medium ripe banana

¾ cup fresh or frozen blueberries

2 cups icy water from the fridge

1 tablespoon ground flax seed

1 tablespoon hemp protein

1 tablespoon raw agave nectar

1 tablespoon omega oil mixture

2 teaspoons fine rooibos tea

DIRECTIONS:

1. Place the banana in the freezer for half an hour after peeling.
2. Place the banana, blueberries and all of the other ingredients into a blender and blend until smooth.
3. Pour into 2 medium sized glasses and serve.

Nutritional Facts per Serving: *Calories 207, Fat 8.8g, Carbs 30.0g, Dietary Fiber 4.7g, Protein 4.8g*

Vegan Athlete Cookbook

LEMON AND LIME TANG

A refreshing drink with a delicious citrus tang! You can easily adjust the flavors of this by using buckwheat sprouts instead of the barley. Yum!

Serves 2

INGREDIENTS:

2 sachets yerba mate tea

1 sachet of green tea

2 cups hot but not boiling water

4 large juicy Medjool dates

1 tablespoon coconut oil

1 tablespoon hemp protein

1 tablespoon white chia seeds

1 tablespoon cooked sprouted barley

½ large fresh lemon, juiced

½ fresh lime juiced

DIRECTIONS:

1. Steep the yerba mate in a cup of hot water for 10 minutes. (longer if you wish to have a stronger flavor)
2. Steep the green tea in a similar amount of water for the time preferred.
3. Remove the tea bags and chill the tea overnight in the refrigerator.
4. The next morning blend the tea with all of the other ingredients in a blender or processor.
5. Serve

Nutritional Facts per Serving: *Calories 160, Fat 8.5g, Carbs 21.2g, Dietary Fiber 4.4g, Protein 4.6g*

101 Flavorful Plant-Based Recipes For Athletic Performance

MANGO CITRUS TINGLE

You will have to taste this to believe how delicious it is! Peppery on your tongue to start your day and an energy boost to run that extra mile!

Serves 2

INGREDIENTS:

1 fresh lime

1 ripe medium sized banana

1 mango peeled and diced

½ habanero pepper

1 cup cold water

1 cup crushed ice

1 tablespoon ground flaxseed

1 tablespoon hemp protein

1½ tablespoons agave nectar

1 tablespoon omega oils

DIRECTIONS:

1. Squeeze the juice from the lime.
2. Peel and chop the banana.
3. Deseed the pepper.
4. Place the fruit along with all of the other ingredients into a blender.
5. Blend for about 30 seconds.
6. Serve.

Nutritional Facts per Serving: *Calories 258, Fat 8.9g, Carbs 44.0g, Dietary Fiber 6.3g, Protein 5.1g*

Vegan Athlete Cookbook

TASTE OF THE TROPICS

So tasty and so good for you, almost too good to be true! Add an extra zing with some granadilla juice to make this even more tropical. Taste the sunshine!

Serves 2

INGREDIENTS:

1 medium sized ripe banana

2 fresh juicy dates - pitted

1 cup iced water

1 cup ice cubes

½ papaya skinned and seeded

1 cup chopped fresh pineapple

1 lime – juiced

1 tablespoon ground flaxseed

1 tablespoon almond oil

DIRECTIONS:

1. Ensure that all of the ingredients are nice and cold.
2. Freeze the peeled banana, pineapple and papaya for half an hour before blending.
3. Place all of the ingredients into a blender and whizz until smooth.
4. Serve

Nutritional Facts per Serving: *Calories 227, Fat 8.3g, Carbs 39.0g, Dietary Fiber 5.7g, Protein 2.9g*

101 Flavorful Plant-Based Recipes For Athletic Performance

GREEN KIWI FRUIT SMOOTH

Enjoy this 'green' drink which is packed full of flavor and vitamins! A delicious smoothie, chock-a-block with fruit and goodness!

Serves 4

INGREDIENTS:

3 kiwi fruits

1 mango

1 cup cube fresh pineapple

1 cup sliced ripe peach

2 ripe bananas

1 teaspoon finely grated fresh ginger

1 cup washed baby spinach (packed)

2 cups apple juice - cold

DIRECTIONS:

1. Freeze the fruits for about an hour.
2. Remove the fruit from the freezer and place in a blender
3. Add the ginger, baby spinach and apple juice
4. Blend well and serve while still icy cold

Nutritional Facts per Serving: *Calories 443, Fat 2.2g, Carbs 111.2g, Dietary Fiber 11.3g, Protein 5.2g*

Vegan Athlete Cookbook

ENERGY BARS & FOOD ON THE RUN

101 Flavorful Plant-Based Recipes For Athletic Performance

VANILLA AND ALMOND BARS

A handy bar to have in the fridge! Grab and Go! Enjoy as a breakfast treat or whenever you feel like an energy pick-me-up.

Makes 4

INGREDIENTS:

4 ounces vanilla rice protein

4 tablespoons almond butter

4 tablespoons ground flaxseed

½ cup water

DIRECTIONS:

1. In a medium sized bowl place the protein and the almond butter and mix to a smooth paste.
2. In a separate bowl mix the ground flax seed and the water.
3. Add the water and flaxseed mixture to the protein and butter and combine well together to form a thick paste.
4. Divide the mixture into four and mold carefully into a bar shape.
5. Wrap each bar in tin foil and place in the fridge to harden.
6. Leave for at least 8 hours or overnight.

Nutritional Facts per Serving: *Calories 248, Fat 11.2g, Carbs 6.6g, Dietary Fiber 5.2g, Protein 28.1g*

Vegan Athlete Cookbook

NUTTY CHOCOLATE PROTEIN BAR

Double up on these delicious bars for a chewy readymade snack! Ideal for a quick breakfast or mid afternoon snack when you feel that your energy levels are on the dip.

Makes 4

INGREDIENTS:

4 ounces chocolate rice protein

4 tablespoons smooth or crunchy peanut butter

4 tablespoons ground flax seed

½ cup water

DIRECTIONS:

1. Stir all of the ingredients together in a bowl until you have a smooth consistency, or slightly chunky if using the crunchy peanut butter.
2. Divide the paste into four fairly equal portions and form into bars.
3. Wrap each bar in foil or plastic wrap and leave for 8 hours or overnight in the fridge to harden
4. Unwrap and serve.

Nutritional Facts per Serving: *Calories 235, Fat 11.6g, Carbs 9.9g, Dietary Fiber 6.4g, Protein 27.6g*

101 Flavorful Plant-Based Recipes For Athletic Performance

PECAN NUT MUNCHIES

A great source of energy for that monster workout! These munchies are great for breakfast, lunch boxes or whenever you fancy a treat.

Makes 6

INGREDIENTS:

3 ounces chocolate rice protein

1 tablespoon ground cinnamon

½ cup chopped pecan nuts

2 tablespoons ground flax seed

2 tablespoons almond butter (or other nut butter)

1 tablespoon non-dairy brownie mix

½ cup unsweetened almond milk

DIRECTIONS:

1. Place all of the ingredients into a large bowl and mix well with a wooden spoon until a thick paste is formed.
2. Divide into six fairly even portions and form into bars.
3. Place the bars in the fridge to harden for a couple of hours.
4. Pre-heat the oven to very hot 400 °F.
5. Place the bars on a foil lined baking sheet and bake for 10 – 12 minutes. Make sure that they do not burn.
6. Remove from the oven and cool.
7. Serve.

Nutritional Facts per Serving: *Calories 179, Fat 11.1g, Carbs 9.6g, Dietary Fiber 4.2g, Protein 13.6g*

Vegan Athlete Cookbook

CINNAMON AND CORN COOKIES

Portable and delicious! Make up a double batch of these so that you have an extra couple on hand.

Makes 2

INGREDIENTS:

1 cup very finely ground cornmeal

1 teaspoon ground cinnamon

2 tablespoons turbinado sugar

Agave nectar to taste

White chia seeds to sprinkle

Water to mix

DIRECTIONS:

1. Pre-heat the oven to 350° F.
2. Prepare a small baking sheet by covering it with non-stick parchment paper.
3. Toast the cornmeal until it is a light brown color in a skillet over a medium heat. This will take about 5 minutes.
4. Cool and transfer to a medium sized bowl.
5. Add the cinnamon and agave nectar.
6. Add some water to the mix, a tablespoon at a time, until an oatmeal-like consistency is reached.
7. Form into 4 small biscuit shapes and place on the baking sheet.
8. Bake for 10 – 15 minutes in the pre-heated oven.
9. When cooked, remove from the oven and cool.

Nutritional Facts per Serving: *Calories 271, Fat 2.0g, Carbs 59.6g, Dietary Fiber 10.8g, Protein 4.1g*

DRIED FRUIT AND COCONUT CHEWS

An athlete's dream chew, jam packed with energy - and tasty too! Change these around with different dried fruits, flavors etc. – whatever takes your fancy and whatever you have in the cupboard.

Makes 12

INGREDIENTS:

1½ cups cooked white beans

½ cup almond butter

¼ cup maple syrup

¼ cup chopped, pitted dates

1 teaspoon almond extract

1 teaspoon ground cinnamon

¼ teaspoon sea salt

1½ cups oats

1 cup whole wheat flour

½ cup dried apricots

½ cup shredded coconut

DIRECTIONS:

1. Pre-heat the oven to 350° F.
2. Grease a 13 x 9 inch pan with a little vegetable oil.
3. Combine the beans, butter, maple syrup, dates, almond extract, cinnamon and salt in a processor until smooth.
4. Add the oats and flour and pulse to combine.
5. Stir in the apricots and coconut.
6. The mixture should be spreadable and if it is a little dry add a few tablespoons of water. If the mixture is too wet add a little more flour.

Vegan Athlete Cookbook

7. Spread the mixture into the prepared pan.
8. Bake for 15 to 20 minutes until toasty brown.
9. Cool in the tin. Cut into squares and serve.

Nutritional Facts per Serving: *Calories 271, Fat 8.0g, Carbs 40.5g, Dietary Fiber 6.4g, Protein 10.8g*

101 Flavorful Plant-Based Recipes For Athletic Performance

BLUEBERRY FLAX GRANOLA

A handful of crunch that will keep for several weeks in an airtight tin! If you do not have dried blueberries, dried cranberries or pomegranate seeds would be a tasty alternative.

Makes 14 Servings

INGREDIENTS:

18 ounces fresh rolled oats

1 cup raw or toasted chopped almonds (nicer if you toast them yourself)

1 cup chopped pecans

1 cup chopped walnuts

¾ cup unsweetened shredded coconut

¼ cup flax seeds

½ teaspoon sea salt

1 teaspoon mixed spice

½ cup maple syrup

½ cup coconut oil

1¼ cups dried blueberries

DIRECTIONS:

1. Pre-heat the oven to 350° F.
2. Prepare a large roasting pan.
3. In a large bowl stir together all of the dry ingredients except the blueberries.
4. In a separate bowl whisk together the maple syrup and coconut oil until well combined.
5. Pour the liquid mixture over the dry ingredients and stir to evenly coat.
6. Spread the granola mixture out on the roasting pan in an even

layer.

7. Bake for 40 – 50 minutes, stirring a few times.
8. Remove from the oven and allow the granola to cool.
9. Add the dried blueberries.
10. When completely cold transfer to an airtight container.
11. The granola will keep for a month.

Nutritional Facts per Serving: *Calories 441, Fat 28.7g, Carbs 38.8g, Dietary Fiber 8.1g, Protein 10.4g*

101 Flavorful Plant-Based Recipes For Athletic Performance

STRAWBERRY ENERGY BAR

Simply delicious and irresistibly good! Try fresh dates instead of dried ones and raspberries instead of strawberries. Whatever you have will be great!

Makes 8

INGREDIENTS:

2 cups soaked dry dates

½ cup roasted carob powder

½ cup hemp protein

½ cup white chia seeds

¾ cup chopped strawberries

½ cup ground flax seed

½ cup sunflower seeds

1 teaspoon lemon or orange zest

2 teaspoons fresh lime juice

Sea salt to taste

1 cup cooked sprouted buckwheat

1 cup frozen strawberries

DIRECTIONS:

1. Place all of the ingredients except the buckwheat and frozen strawberries into a processor.
2. Process to a smooth paste.
3. Gradually knead in the buckwheat and frozen strawberries with your hands.
4. Shape into bars and serve

Nutritional Facts per Serving: *Calories 297, Fat 8.0g, Carbs 50.1g, Dietary Fiber 13.2g, Protein 12.3g*

Vegan Athlete Cookbook

CRUNCHY GRANOLA BARS

Granola in a bar! So simple to make too. Wrap these in plastic wrap or foil and add to your pocket as you leave for a training session!

Makes 12

INGREDIENTS:

1 can chickpeas which have been rinsed and drained

2 teaspoons cinnamon powder

2 teaspoons natural brown sugar

1½ cups oatmeal

1 cup brown rice crispie cereal

1 cup chopped mixed dried fruit

½ cup peanut butter

¼ cup maple syrup

3 tablespoons coconut oil

1 tablespoon ground flax seed

Warm water

DIRECTIONS:

1. Pre-heat the oven to 375°F.
2. Prepare a baking sheet and an 8 x 8 greased glass or ceramic dish.
3. Mix the ground flax seed with ¼ cup warm water. Set aside.
4. Toss the chickpeas in the brown sugar and 1 teaspoon of cinnamon.
5. Toast the chickpeas and sugar mixture in the oven on the baking sheet for about 20 minutes, stirring half way through the cooking time.
6. Add the oatmeal to the pan and bake for a further 5 minutes or

101 Flavorful Plant-Based Recipes For Athletic Performance

    so until toasty. Remove from the oven.

7. Add the cereal, dried fruits and the rest of the cinnamon to the chickpea/oatmeal mixture.

8. Stir together the peanut butter, maple syrup, coconut oil and the flax mixture.

9. Pour the wet ingredients over the dry ingredients and stir well to combine.

10. Press the mixture well into the greased dish and refrigerate when cool.

11. When the mixture is firm cut into 12 small bars.

Nutritional Facts per Serving: *Calories 217, Fat 10.0g, Carbs 28.7g, Dietary Fiber 3.8g, Protein 5.7g*

CHOCOLATE COCONUT QUINOA SLICES

Chocolate and coconut – taste sensation indeed! Crunch, munch, silence... Yum!

Makes 12

INGREDIENTS:

¾ cup quinoa

½ cup dried chopped dates

3 tablespoons maple syrup

2 tablespoons olive oil

2 tablespoons ground flaxseed

½ teaspoon almond extract

¼ teaspoon salt

½ cup chocolate protein powder

½ cup whole wheat flour

¼ cup Vegan chocolate chips

¼ cup shredded coconut

Water

DIRECTIONS:

1. Pre-heat the oven to 350°F.
2. Prepare an 8 x 8 ovenproof baking dish. Grease lightly with oil.
3. Rinse the quinoa in cold water and leave to soak for about 10 minutes.
4. Drain the quinoa. Place 1 cup of water in a small sauce pan bring to the boil. Add the quinoa and simmer over a low heat for about 12 minutes. Cool.
5. In a food processor combine the cooked quinoa, dates, maple syrup, olive oil, flaxseed, almond extract and salt.

101 Flavorful Plant-Based Recipes For Athletic Performance

6. Process until fairly smooth.
7. In a separate bowl stir together the chocolate protein powder, flour chocolate chips and coconut.
8. Fold the dry mixture into the wet mixture with a flat spatula or knife.
9. Press into the prepared baking dish. Even out the top.
10. Bake for about 25 minutes, until firm.
11. Cool and then slice into bars.
12. Store in an airtight container for about a week or freeze up to 3 months.

Nutritional Facts per Serving: *Calories 160, Fat 4.7g, Carbs 22.4g, Dietary Fiber 2.9g, Protein 9.0g*

Vegan Athlete Cookbook

APPLE AND NUT CHEWS

Full of wholefood goodness and nutty flavor! These can be toasted for an extra taste dimension!

Makes 24

INGREDIENTS:

½ cup whole wheat flour

¾ cup oats

1 cup grape nuts cereal

¾ cup golden raisins

1 cup shredded coconut (sweetened or unsweetened)

¼ cup raw almonds

½ cup raw cashews

2 teaspoons ground cinnamon

2 tablespoons ground flax seeds

¼ cup warm water

15 ounce can Great Northern Beans

1 cup chopped fresh dates

1 teaspoon vanilla extract

2 tablespoons maple syrup or brown sugar

1 tablespoon vegetable oil

½ cup apple sauce

DIRECTIONS:

1. Preheat your oven to 350° F.
2. Grease a 9 x 13 oven dish
3. Wash and drain the beans to remove any salt. Chop roughly.

101 Flavorful Plant-Based Recipes For Athletic Performance

4. Mix the flaxseed with the warm water and set aside to thicken.
5. Combine the flour, oats, grape not cereal, raisins, coconut, nuts and cinnamon in a large bowl.
6. Mix the beans, flaxseed mix, dates, vanilla, maple syrup, oil and apple sauce together and add to the dry ingredients.
7. Mix well.
8. Press into the prepared oven dish.
9. Bake for about 25 minutes, rotating the dish after 15 minutes.
10. Remove from the oven and cool.
11. Cut into 24 small bars.
12. Either leave unwrapped for hard chewier bars or wrap for a softer texture.
13. These will keep for about a week unfrozen. Freeze them if you want to keep them for longer.

Nutritional Facts per Serving: *Calories 138, Fat 4.1g, Carbs 23.8g, Dietary Fiber 3.4g, Protein 3.7g*

Vegan Athlete Cookbook

BANANA CAROB BARS WITH A CHILI TWIST

As easy as pie to make – you'll just love that banana tang! Store in the fridge wrapped or in an airtight container. Enjoy.

Makes 8

INGREDIENTS:

¼ cup Medjool dates

½ jalapeno pepper

1 small ripe banana

½ cup cooked buckwheat

¼ cup roasted carob powder

¼ cup white chia seeds

¼ cup roasted macadamia nuts

Pinch of sea salt

Raw sesame seeds to sprinkle

DIRECTIONS:

1. Place all of the ingredients into a food processor.
2. Process by pulsing until all of the ingredients are well mixed and have come together.
3. Press into 8 small bars or round cakes if you prefer.
4. Sprinkle with sesame seeds.

Nutritional Facts per Serving: *Calories 90, Fat 4.4g, Carbs 13.4g, Dietary Fiber 3.3g, Protein 2.0g*

101 Flavorful Plant-Based Recipes For Athletic Performance

ENERGY BARS THE VEGAN WAY

Need a pick me up? These bars are just right for that energy sapped moment! An energetic taste sensation that is sure to please.

Makes 12

INGREDIENTS:

½ cup pumpkin seeds

1½ cups water

2 cups dried chopped figs

4 scoops vanilla rice protein

12 tablespoons Vegan dark chocolate chips

1 tablespoon coconut oil

Sea salt to taste

12 whole almonds

DIRECTIONS:

1. Blend the pumpkin seeds and water until smooth in a blender.
2. Add the figs and the protein powder and blend once more until smooth.
3. Flatten the mixture onto a freezer proof cookie sheet and freeze until firm. About half an hour.
4. While the bars are freezing melt the chocolate chips in the top of a double boiler or in a heatproof bowl on top of a saucepan of simmering water.
5. Spread the ½ of the chocolate mixture over the fig mixture top with the whole almonds and place back in the freezer for another 15 minutes or so.
6. Add the coconut oil to the rest of the melted chocolate and drizzle over the fig mixture and almonds.
7. Cut the mixture into bars and sprinkle with sea salt as desired.

Vegan Athlete Cookbook

8. Refrigerate until ready to eat.

Nutritional Facts per Serving: *Calories 240, Fat 8.7g, Carbs 33.8g, Dietary Fiber 4.3g, Protein 11.8g*

101 Flavorful Plant-Based Recipes For Athletic Performance

NOODLES, QUINOA AND RICE

Vegan Athlete Cookbook

RAW PAD THAI

Kelp noodles and a variety of vegetables make up this Thai style dish.

Serves 4

INGREDIENTS:

1 pound kelp noodles

Lukewarm water

1 cup lemon juice

3 tablespoons nut butter

1 large carrot - grated

3 cups mixed lettuce greens

1 cup chopped peanuts

1 red bell pepper – chopped

Liquid aminos to taste

Pinch cayenne pepper

DIRECTIONS:

1. Soak the kelp noodles in ½ cup of lemon juice and some luke warm water for about 30 minutes. Drain.
2. Meanwhile make a sauce by blending together the rest of the lemon juice, aminos, nut butter, cayenne pepper with enough water to make a sauce-like consistency.
3. Taste the sauce and add some more aminos or lemon juice according to your taste.
4. Pour the sauce into a large bowl and mix in the prepared drained noodles, prepared vegetables and the peanuts.
5. Serve and enjoy.

Nutritional Facts per Serving: *Calories 316, Fat 24.7g, Carbs 39.0g, Dietary Fiber 7.3g, Protein 12.6g*

HERBED QUINOA AND HEMP

A tasty quinoa dish to serve on its own or with a bean stew! Add some variety by using different herbs and perhaps some chili powder instead of the turmeric.

Serves 2

INGREDIENTS:

1 cup quinoa

2 tablespoons hemp seeds

Water

Sea salt and freshly ground black pepper

¼ teaspoon turmeric

¼ teaspoon dried oregano

¼ teaspoon dried basil

1 tablespoon olive oil

2 tablespoons hummus

DIRECTIONS:

1. In a medium sized saucepan simmer together the quinoa, hemp seeds and water until tender – about 20 minutes.
2. Add the spices and herbs.
3. Stir in the olive oil and hummus.

Nutritional Facts per Serving: *Calories 245, Fat 27.2g, Carbs 59.6g, Dietary Fiber 8.6g, Protein 22.4g*

Vegan Athlete Cookbook

BEAN BALL SPAGHETTI

Delicious tomato covered bean balls. Delish! Add some chili to the marinara sauce for a different flavor and use a different type of pasta or rice noodle for a change. These smell superb as they are cooking.

Serves 6

INGREDIENTS:

2 x 15 ounce cans pinto beans

1 large minced carrot

½ cup very finely chopped parsley

Garlic flakes or fresh garlic minced

½ cup whole wheat bread crumbs

1 tablespoon olive oil

1½ tablespoons mixed Italian herb seasoning

Sea salt and freshly ground black pepper

3 generous cups marinara sauce

Spaghetti to serve

DIRECTIONS:

1. Preheat the oven to 375°F.
2. Line a cookie sheet with parchment paper.
3. In a food processor combine the carrot, parsley, garlic, herbs, bread crumbs, oil, seasoning and drained beans.
4. Process until the mixture is sticky. Add more seasoning if desired.
5. Form the mixture into small balls about the size of a walnut. Dampen your hands with water if the mixture sticks.
6. Place apart on the prepared cookie sheet and bake for about 20 minutes until brown.

101 Flavorful Plant-Based Recipes For Athletic Performance

7. While the bean balls are cooking, heat the marinara sauce in a large saucepan.
8. Add the browned balls to the sauce and simmer together for about 10 minutes until the flavors are well combined.
9. Serve over cooked spaghetti.

Nutritional Facts per Serving (not including spaghetti): *Calories 665, Fat 8.7g, Carbs 112.8g, Dietary Fiber 26.3g, Protein 33.7g*

Vegan Athlete Cookbook

MUSHROOM SPIRALS

This recipe is a wonderful standby when guests arrive and an easy recipe to double or triple quantities depending on the number you wish to serve – there certainly won't be any left!

Serves 4

INGREDIENTS:

12 ounces dried whole wheat rotini or fusilli

3 tablespoons olive oil

8 ounces brown mushrooms

5 cloves garlic - finely chopped

1 large onion, finely sliced

1½ tablespoons finely chopped mixed herbs

½ teaspoon cayenne pepper

½ cup vegetable stock

½ cup dry white wine

¼ cup Dijon mustard

¼ cup pine nuts

Sea salt to taste

DIRECTIONS:

1. Slice the mushrooms and cook until tender in half of the olive oil. Place in a large bowl and set aside.

2. In the same pan add the rest of the oil and fry the garlic and onion until soft. Add the mixed herbs and the cayenne pepper.

3. Add the stock to the onion mixture and bring to the boil. Simmer for a couple of minutes. Add to the mushrooms in the bowl.

4. In the same pan add the wine and mustard and mix well

101 Flavorful Plant-Based Recipes For Athletic Performance

   together scraping the bottom of the pan to pick up all of the onion and mushroom flavor that may still be there.

5. Once boiling, add the mushrooms and onions and simmer very gently together while you are cooking the pasta.
6. Cook the pasta according to the directions on the packet. Drain well and add to the mushroom sauce.
7. Serve in bowls. Sprinkle with pine nuts.

Nutritional Facts per Serving: *Calories 522, Fat 18.1g, Carbs 73.5g, Dietary Fiber 5.4g, Protein 15.1g*

Vegan Athlete Cookbook

MACARONI AND VEGETABLES

Use a different pasta shape if you do not have macaroni – just as long as it has lots of crevasses and twists for the delicious sauce to cling to!

Serves 4 generously

INGREDIENTS:

12 ounces elbow macaroni

1 bunch Swiss chard

3 tablespoons vegetable oil

2 finely chopped garlic cloves

1 medium potato, peeled and chunked

2 generous cups vegetable stock

Salt and pepper to taste

½ teaspoon turmeric

¾ teaspoon powdered paprika

¼ cup roasted cashew nuts

¼ cup roasted pine nuts

I tablespoon freshly squeezed lemon juice

1 teaspoon Dijon mustard

½ cup dried whole wheat bread crumbs

DIRECTIONS:

1. Pre-heat the oven to 350°F.
2. Prepare a baking dish 9 x 13 inches by lightly oiling it.
3. Remove the ribs from the chard, rinse very well and steam for about 5 minutes until tender. Set aside to cool.
4. When cool squeeze all of the excess water from the cooked chard.

101 Flavorful Plant-Based Recipes For Athletic Performance

5. In a large sauce pan, heat 2 tablespoons of the oil over a medium heat. When hot add the onion, garlic and potato. Season and cover with a lid. Cook until all of the vegetables are tender. About 8 minutes.

6. Add the stock to the potatoes and onion mixture together with the turmeric and paprika and continue cooking until the vegetables are quite soft. Stir in the lemon juice and the mustard.

7. Leave the potatoes one side to cool.

8. Blend the cashews and pine nuts until a fine powder. Add the potatoes, onion and stock mixture and blend all together until smooth.

9. Season to taste.

10. Cook the macaroni in plenty of salted boiling water until tender. Drain well.

11. Combine the cooked macaroni with the potato mixture and the Swiss chard and spoon into the prepared baking dish.

12. Sprinkle with the breadcrumbs. And drizzle with the remaining tablespoon of oil.

13. Bake in the hot oven for about half an hour until brown and sizzling.

14. Serve.

Nutritional Facts per Serving: *Calories 647, Fat 23.4g, Carbs 88.6g, Dietary Fiber 6.8g, Protein 19.4g*

GARLICKY BEAN PASTA

A taste sensation! Try this with different herbs and maybe a touch of lime juice instead of the lemon.

Serves 8

INGREDIENTS:

2 x 15 ounce cans of white beans

6 tablespoons olive oil

4 fresh cloves of garlic finely chopped

Juice of 1 lemon

2 tablespoons fresh oregano or marjoram

1 teaspoon fresh basil

24 ounces dried linguine, fettuccine or trenette pasta

Plenty of chopped parsley

Salt and pepper

DIRECTIONS:

1. Cook the pasta according to the instructions on the packet.
2. Reserve a cupful of the cooking water once the pasta is cooked.
3. In the meantime, heat the oil in pan over a medium heat.
4. Sauté the garlic briefly making sure it does not burn.
5. Add the drained beans, lemon juice, herbs and the pasta water. Season to taste.
6. Toss in the pasta and plenty of chopped parsley.
7. Serve while hot.

Nutritional Facts per Serving: *Calories 692, Fat 13.5g, Carbs 111.3g, Dietary Fiber 16.6g, Protein 34.6g*

QUINOA AND BRAISED MIXED VEGETABLES

A fabulous recipe to use up all those odd vegetables that you have left in the fridge just before shopping day! This is wonderful with chunks of crispy homemade whole wheat bread to soak up all of the juices.

Serves 6

INGREDIENTS:

2 tablespoons olive oil

2/3 cup quinoa

1 diced carrot

1 small red onion finely chopped

1 small head cauliflower broken into florets

½ Bell pepper seeded and chopped

3 crushed cloves garlic

2 cups homemade vegetable stock

1 large can whole peeled chopped tomatoes

4 tablespoons juice from the canned tomatoes

1½ cups sliced Bok Choi

10 torn basil leaves

2 bay leaves

2 teaspoons Italian mixed herbs

2 cups baby spinach

Salt and freshly ground pepper to taste

Plenty of chopped parsley to serve

DIRECTIONS:

1. Heat the oil in a large saucepan over a medium high heat.
2. Put the quinoa, carrot, onion, pepper, cauliflower and garlic

into the pan and stir.

3. Stir fry for a few minutes until just beginning to turn brown.
4. Pour in the stock along with 2½ cups of water, the chopped tomatoes, tomato sauce, cabbage, and all of the seasonings.
5. Increase the heat to high and bring everything to the boil.
6. Once boiling, reduce the heat to medium low and simmer until the stew is tender. This will take about 10 minutes or so.
7. Season to taste, remove the bay leaves and serve while hot.

Nutritional Facts per Serving: *Calories 141, Fat 6.0g, Carbs 18.7g, Dietary Fiber 4.1g, Protein 4.6g*

101 Flavorful Plant-Based Recipes For Athletic Performance

PIZZA PERFECT

Vegan Athlete Cookbook

BEAN AND TOMATO PIZZA

Saturday night is pizza night! Or, actually, with this healthy version, any night you fancy! Share with family and friends – they will be asking for more.

Serves 4

INGREDIENTS:

2¾ cups plain all-purpose flour

2½ teaspoons instant yeast

1 teaspoon salt

1 cup lukewarm water

1 tablespoon olive oil

4 cloves garlic finely chopped

1 x 15 ounce can cannellini beans

¼ teaspoon salt

¼ teaspoon freshly ground black pepper

¼ cup vegetable stock

3 tablespoons torn fresh basil

3 ripe medium tomatoes, sliced

DIRECTIONS:

1. Prepare a baking sheet by covering with sifted flour. You could use a pizza stone if you have one.
2. In a large bowl, combine the flour, yeast, salt and lukewarm water. Stir until well combined and a soft dough is formed. Add more water if necessary, a little at a time.
3. Turn the dough onto a floured surface and knead for about 10 minutes until smooth and elastic. This could also be done with the dough hook on a mixer if you have one.

101 Flavorful Plant-Based Recipes For Athletic Performance

4. Shape the dough into a ball, place in an oiled bowl, and cover with plastic wrap and leave until doubled in size – about 1 hour in a warm room.

5. When the dough has risen, knead it very gently on a floured board and place this on the prepared baking tray. Do not worry if it is not perfect!

6. Let the dough rise again for another 20 minutes or so.

7. Pre-heat the oven to 425°F.

8. While the dough is rising for the second time and the oven is getting hot, prepare the topping.

9. In a large skillet fry the garlic until soft in the olive oil. Add the drained and washed beans, salt and pepper.

10. When the mixture is warm, mash the beans with a potato masher and stir in the vegetable stock.

11. Simmer for about 10 minutes until the mixture is nice and creamy and thick. Stir in the torn basil.

12. When the pizza has risen top the dough with the bean mixture, spreading it evenly to within about ¾ inch from the edge.

13. Arrange the tomato slices neatly on top and season with salt and pepper.

14. Bake in the hot oven on the lowest shelf for about 15 minutes until cooked and brown.

15. Cut into slices and serve hot.

Nutritional Facts per Serving: *Calories 1057, Fat 5.5g, Carbs 217.3g, Dietary Fiber 30.9g, Protein 29.4g*

Vegan Athlete Cookbook

VEGETABLE PIZZA ON A BEET AND SUNFLOWER SEED CRUST

This interesting version of a pizza is bang full of vitamins and energy giving vegetables!

Serves 4

INGREDIENTS:

2 cups sunflower seeds – ground finely

1 cup grated raw beetroot

¼ cup coconut oil

Sea salt

½ Teaspoon finely chopped parsley

4 generous tablespoons tomato sauce

I sliced tomato

½ red onion finely sliced

1 cup chopped celery

½ cup torn fresh basil

½ cup grated carrot

½ cup sliced spring onions

DIRECTIONS:

1. Pre-heat the oven to 300°F.
2. Lightly oil a baking sheet with coconut oil.
3. Place the sunflower seed, beetroot, coconut oil, salt and parsley in a food processor and pulse until the mixture starts to come together.
4. Spread the mixture onto the prepared tray in a circle or square until it is about ¼ inch thick.
5. Spread the tomato sauce over the base.

101 Flavorful Plant-Based Recipes For Athletic Performance

6. Place the cut tomato, red onion, celery, basil, carrot and spring onion on the top in an even layer.
7. Bake on the top shelf of the oven until brown and crispy – about 35 – 40 minutes.
8. Remove the pizza from the oven. Cut into portions, serve and enjoy.

Nutritional Facts per Serving: *Calories 291, Fat 25.7g, Carbs 13.4g, Dietary Fiber 4.5g, Protein 6.4g*

Vegan Athlete Cookbook

ADZUKI BEAN PIZZA

This recipe contains dulse flakes and strips for a wonderful smoky, salty flavor. A popular pizza that goes great with rest and a remote. You can't work out all the time!

Serves 4

INGREDIENTS:

1 cup cooked adzuki beans

1 cup cooked quinoa

½ cup ground sesame seeds

¼ cup olive oil

2 tablespoons dulse flakes

4 generous tablespoons spicy sun dried tomato pesto

1 small sliced cucumber – seeds removed

½ red onion diced

4 strips dulse

¾ cup bean sprouts

½ cup torn basil pieces

½ cup chopped spring onions

Salt and pepper

DIRECTIONS:

1. Preheat the oven to 300°F.
2. Prepare a baking sheet by lightly oiling with coconut oil.
3. Place the beans, quinoa, sesame seeds, olive oil and dulse flakes in a food processor and pulse until the mixture starts to form a ball.
4. Spread this mixture into a round of even thickness on the prepared baking tray – about a ¼ of an inch.

101 Flavorful Plant-Based Recipes For Athletic Performance

5. Spread with the sun dried tomato pesto and add the sliced cucumber, onions, dulse strips, bean sprouts and basil.
6. Season to taste.
7. Bake for about 40 minutes.
8. When the pizza is crispy remove from the oven.
9. Cut into wedges and enjoy.

Nutritional Facts per Serving: *Calories 773, Fat 46.0g, Carbs 65.5g, Dietary Fiber 13.8g, Protein 27.1g*

TOFU AND TEMPEH

101 Flavorful Plant-Based Recipes For Athletic Performance

SLOPPY JOES

These sloppy concoctions have a wonderful sweet and sour flavor!

Serves 2

INGREDIENTS:

1 cup natural mineral water

1 cup tomato paste mixed with fruit juice

2 tablespoons molasses

2 tablespoons apple cider vinegar

½ cup chopped onion

½ cup chopped green bell pepper

2 tablespoons lemon juice

1 teaspoon mustard powder

1 tablespoon olive oil

½ cup chopped pineapple

4 ounces tempeh

2 whole wheat buns

DIRECTIONS:

1. Sauté the chopped onion and green pepper in a little olive oil in a skillet.
2. Break up the tempeh with a fork and add to the pan and brown.
3. In a small sauce pan heat together the water, tomato paste, molasses, vinegar, lemon juice, mustard powder and pineapple.
4. Add to the tempeh and onion/pepper mixture.
5. Serve over the sliced buns (toasted first if you wish).

Nutritional Facts per Serving: *Calories 525, Fat 15.8g, Carbs 79.1g, Dietary Fiber 9.6g, Protein 22.1g*

Vegan Athlete Cookbook

TOFU WITH SUGAR SNAP PEAS

The crunchy texture of the sugar snap peas combines beautifully with the velvety smoothness of the tofu! Savor the flavor – what a wonderful combination this is.

Serves 6

INGREDIENTS:

21 ounces extra-firm tofu

2 teaspoons olive oil

¾ pound soba noodles

1½ cups trimmed sugar snap peas

2 teaspoons curry paste (as hot as you dare)

¾ cup coconut milk

3 tablespoons fresh lime juice

1½ teaspoons brown sugar

3 tablespoons Vegan soya sauce

¾ cup smooth peanut butter

Salt

DIRECTIONS:

1. Cut the tofu into cubes and leave to drain to remove any excess water. This will take about 15 minutes.

2. Blanch the trimmed sugar snap peas in lightly salted boiling water for 30 seconds. Leave to cool.

3. Cook the soba noodles according to the directions on the packet. When done, drain and rinse the noodles in cold water.

4. Set a large skillet on a medium to high heat and add the olive oil to it. Heat the oil.

5. Add the tofu cubes to the skillet and toss gently to brown lightly

101 Flavorful Plant-Based Recipes For Athletic Performance

on all sides. Sprinkle with salt and set aside.

6. Keep the skillet to one side whilst you prepare the sauce by whisking together the peanut butter and coconut milk in a small saucepan over a medium heat.
7. Add the curry paste, lime juice, soy sauce and the brown sugar.
8. Place the curried coconut milk mixture into the skillet.
9. Add the tofu, noodles and peas.
10. Heat gently all together for a few minutes so that the flavors combine.
11. Serve in bowls so that you do not lose all of the juices.

Nutritional Facts per Serving: *Calories 578, Fat 32.1g, Carbs 55.2g, Dietary Fiber 3.4g, Protein 27.7g*

Vegan Athlete Cookbook

TEMPEH WITH A NUTTY SAUCE

Spicy tempeh with a fresh vegetable sauce! Add different vegetables or nuts – it is up to you!

Serves 4

INGREDIENTS:

8 ounces tempeh - diced

5 tablespoons soy sauce

1 teaspoon finely chopped garlic

3 teaspoons freshly grated ginger

2 tablespoons vegetable oil

1 large cucumber, peeled, seeded and chopped

1 yellow bell pepper, chopped

8 scallions, thinly sliced

¼ cup finely chopped peanuts

1 4oz packet rice noodles

¼ cup smooth peanut butter

2 tablespoons rice vinegar

1 tablespoon dry sherry

1 tablespoon maple syrup

1 tablespoon sesame oil

1 teaspoon curry paste

Sea salt and freshly ground black pepper to taste

DIRECTIONS:

1. Mix the diced tempeh, 3 tablespoons of the soy sauce, ginger and garlic in a bowl. Leave for the flavors to infuse for about 15 minutes.

101 Flavorful Plant-Based Recipes For Athletic Performance

2. Soak the noodles in warm water for about 15 minutes until tender.

3. Whisk together 2 tablespoon of soy sauce, peanut butter, sherry, maple syrup, sesame oil and curry paste in a bowl. Set aside.

4. Heat 1 tablespoon of vegetable oil in a skillet and lightly brown the tempeh. Stir every so often to ensure even browning. Transfer to a small bowl and keep warm when done.

5. Heat the remaining tablespoon of oil in the skillet and cook the cucumber, half the bell pepper and half of the scallions until al dente.

6. Season with just a little salt and pepper.

7. Mix in the tempeh and sauce and serve over the cooked noodles.

8. Sprinkle with the remaining bell pepper, scallions and the chopped peanuts.

Nutritional Facts per Serving: *Calories 446, Fat 30.1g, Carbs 29.3g, Dietary Fiber 4.1g, Protein 20.0g*

TEMPEH WITH BLACK BEAN SAUCE

Ever craved for that elusive umami flavor? This could be where you find it! Served over rice or noodles, both ways are exquisite!

Serves 4

INGREDIENTS:

1 pound tempeh, cut into ¾ inch cubes

1 tablespoon corn-starch

¼ cup vegetable stock

1 tablespoon black bean sauce

1 teaspoon brown sugar

4 tablespoons peanut oil

¼ teaspoon dried chili flakes

Small head of fresh kale

2 small zucchinis

1 yellow bell pepper cut into strips

4 ounces of sugar snap peas

Soy sauce to taste

DIRECTIONS:

1. Whisk together the cornstarch and vegetable stock and sugar, Mix all well together.
2. Heat 3 tablespoons of the peanut oil in a skillet over a high heat. When the oil is hot add the tempeh cubes and brown them quickly on all sides. Be careful that they are hot but do not burn!
3. Remove the tempeh from the skillet and drain on paper towel.
4. Wipe the skillet with paper towel to clean and then add the other tablespoon of oil.

101 Flavorful Plant-Based Recipes For Athletic Performance

5. When the oil is hot add all of the vegetables and stir fry for about 3 minutes – they must still be crisp.
6. Return the tempeh to the skillet and stir everything together for a short while until heated through. Do not let the tempeh stick!
7. Season with soy sauce to taste.
8. Serve.

Nutritional Facts per Serving: *Calories 391, Fat 26.2g, Carbs 21.5g, Dietary Fiber 2.2g, Protein 23.1g*

Vegan Athlete Cookbook

CURRIED TOFU

Tofu with a tomato, Thai flavor. What a pleasure! This can be made hotter with the addition of another spoonful or two of the red curry paste.

Serves 6

INGREDIENTS:

3 tablespoons peanut oil

1 pint halved cherry tomatoes

2 14 ounce cartons extra-firm tofu cut into cubes

1 red onion, very thinly sliced

2 ¼ cups coconut milk

1 tablespoon Thai red curry paste

Soy sauce to season

½ cup torn basil

½ cup chopped mint

Salt

DIRECTIONS:

1. Heat a tablespoon of oil in a skillet over a medium high heat. When hot add the tomatoes and stir fry quickly until tender but not mushy. This will take about 2 minutes. Sprinkle with a little salt.
2. Put the tomatoes in a clean bowl and set to one side.
3. Wipe the skillet with kitchen towel and add a little more of the oil. Add the tofu cubes in batches and fry on all sides until golden brown.
4. Remove the tofu from the pan and sprinkle with some salt. Set aside.
5. Add some more of the oil to the pan and sauté the onion until lightly brown.

101 Flavorful Plant-Based Recipes For Athletic Performance

6. Add the coconut milk and the curry paste to the onions in the pan and mix well together. Simmer for a shirt while until the mixture thickens a little.

7. Add the tofu back into the pan and leave for a couple of minutes to warm through. Add soy sauce to taste.

8. Finally add the herbs and the tomatoes.

9. Serve with rice or noodles or a baked potato

Nutritional Facts per Serving: *Calories 417, Fat 36.8g, Carbs 12.4g, Dietary Fiber 4.0g, Protein 16.0g*

Vegan Athlete Cookbook

KOREAN TOFU SALAD

A mystical touch of the Far East with a vegetable and ginger tang! Excellent on a warm summer's day.

Serves 4

INGREDIENTS:

1 pound extra-firm tofu

½ cup soy sauce

5 cups finely shredded cabbage

3 finely chopped spring onions

3 finely chopped garlic cloves

1 tablespoon brown sugar

1 teaspoon chili paste

¼ cup rice vinegar

3 tablespoons sesame oil

4 tablespoons water

DIRECTIONS:

1. Pre-heat the oven to 375°F. Line a baking sheet with parchment and oil lightly.

2. Cut the tofu into ½ cubes and press to remove excess water.

3. Toss the tofu with half of the soy sauce. Arrange the cubes on the baking tray and bake for about half an hour in the oven. Remove from the oven and set aside to cool.

4. In a large bowl combine the shredded cabbage, carrots and onions. Set to one side.

5. In a small bowl mix together the garlic, brown sugar, chili paste, the rest of the soy sauce, vinegar, sesame oil and water.

6. Pour this mixture over the cabbage and toss to dress. Season to

taste.

7. Leave the cabbage to one side for about 3
8. Serve topped with the tofu.

Nutritional Facts per Serving: *Calories 262, Fat 17.1g, ... 14.1g, Dietary Fiber 3.2g, Protein 14.8g*

Vegan Athlete Cookbook

SWEET POTATO CURRY WITH CARAMELIZED SHALLOTS

The shallots give a wonderful sweetness to this sweet potato and tofu curry! Try serving with pasta for a different take on this recipe.

Serves 4

INGREDIENTS:

1 pound sweet potatoes

1 x 15 ounce can coconut milk

2 teaspoons Thai red curry paste

½ cup chopped cilantro plus extra to garnish

1 x 14 ounce carton extra-firm tofu drained and cut into 1 inch cubes

1 tablespoon roasted peanut oil

Mushroom soy sauce to season

7 large shallots thinly sliced

6 baby Bok Choy cut in quarters

1 lime, quartered

Brown Basmati rice to serve

DIRECTIONS:

1. Put the rice on the stove to cook.
2. Cut the sweet potatoes into wedges and steam them for about 20 minutes until tender.
3. Warm the coconut milk with a cup of water in a skillet. Stir in the curry paste and cilantro.
4. Add the cooked sweet potato and lower the heat to a simmer.
5. Place in a separate bowl when cooked.
6. Put the tofu in a single layer in the skillet over medium heat.
7. Cook until the water has evaporated and the tofu is golden,

101 Flavorful Plant-Based Recipes For Athletic Performance

about 5 minutes, adding a little oil for flavor and to give it a crisp surface.

8. Season with salt, douse with a few teaspoons mushroom soy sauce
9. Turn the tofu cubes until they are coated evenly and a dark golden brown.
10. When brown, add the tofu to the sweet potatoes, wipe out the pan, and return it to the heat.
11. Add 2 teaspoons of the remaining oil to the skillet. When hot add the shallots, season with salt and cook until caramelized. Set aside.
12. Simmer the Bok Choy in salted water until tender. Drain and toss with the rest of the ingredients.
13. Toss everything with the remaining oil.
14. Serve the sweet potatoes with their sauce over cooked rice.

Nutritional Facts per Serving (not including rice): *Calories 657, Fat 35.5g, Carbs 70.2g, Dietary Fiber 20.5g, Protein 31.7g*

BEANS, PEAS AND LENTILS

101 Flavorful Plant-Based Recipes For Athletic Performance

LENTILS AND VEGGIES WITH A ZIP

A complete protein meal for the family! Change the choice of vegetables and lentils to give a good variety of meals using this simple method.

Serves 4

INGREDIENTS:

2 cups fresh baby spinach

½ cup torn fresh basil

2 cups baby carrots

2 ripe tomatoes

4 cups cauliflower florets

4 cups lentils of your choice

½ teaspoon of each of: garlic, turmeric and dried oregano

4 tablespoons hemp seeds

2 tablespoons mixed omega oils

DIRECTIONS:

1. Wash and clean the vegetables well and rinse the lentils to remove any grit.
2. Steam the vegetables for about 30 minutes until tender.
3. Cook the lentils in plenty of salted water until tender – about 30 minutes.
4. Combine the vegetables, lentils, garlic, turmeric and dried oregano.
5. Stir in the hempseeds and the oils.

Nutritional Facts per Serving: *Calories 962, Fat 25.4g, Carbs 131.5g, Dietary Fiber 35.1g, Protein 65.5g*

Vegan Athlete Cookbook

RED LENTILS WITH AN INDIAN FLAVOR

An easy supper dish with a delicate flavor of whole spices! Make this lentil curry hotter if you like by adding more chilies!

Serves 4

INGREDIENTS:

1½ cups red lentils

Salt to taste

½ teaspoon powdered turmeric

½ teaspoon chili powder

1 tablespoon vegetable oil

2 dried red chilies

1 teaspoon panch phoran – spice mix

DIRECTIONS:

1. Wash the lentils in plenty of running water to clean.
2. In a large sauce pan bring 4 pints of water to the boil and add the lentils, salt, turmeric and chili powder.
3. Simmer over a moderate heat until the lentils are tender – about 25 minutes.
4. Heat the oil in a small pan and fry the red chilies and the panch phoran spice mix for about 20 seconds to release their flavor.
5. Pour the flavored oil over the lentils.
6. Stir well and adjust the seasoning.
7. The lentil curry should be thick but if too thick at some boiled water from a kettle to loosen it a little.

Nutritional Facts per Serving: *Calories 286, Fat 4.2g, Carbs 43.6g, Dietary Fiber 22.1g, Protein 18.6g*

101 Flavorful Plant-Based Recipes For Athletic Performance

PISTACHIOS AND BEANS

This is a complete protein meal with black beans and the pistachios. The omega oils add a roundness to the taste and health boost this meal gives.

Serves 4

INGREDIENTS:

2 cups fresh basil leaves – torn

2 cups chunked red bell peppers

2 cups chunked yellow bell peppers

2 cups broccoli florets

4 cups cooked black beans

½ teaspoon ground cumin

½ teaspoon ground ginger

½ teaspoon dried oregano

½ cup chopped pistachios

2 tablespoons mixed omega oil

DIRECTIONS:

1. Steam the vegetables for about 30 minutes until tender.
2. Add in the spices to the vegetables.
3. Mix with the cooked beans and add the pistachios.
4. Drizzle over the oil and lightly combine.

Nutritional Facts per Serving: *Calories 848, Fat 17.0g, Carbs 131.9g, Dietary Fiber 33.4g, Protein 47.0g*

Vegan Athlete Cookbook

NUTTY BEAN CROQUETTES

Perfect for a quick lunch, with a crispy green side salad!

Serves 4

INGREDIENTS:

¼ cup roughly chopped walnuts

4 green onions, chopped

4 tablespoons coarsely chopped parsley

1 cup cooked black beans

1 tablespoon soy sauce

½ cup wheat gluten flour

2 teaspoons chopped fresh savory

Sea salt and freshly ground black pepper

¾ cup dried breadcrumbs

2 tablespoons olive oil

DIRECTIONS:

1. Combine the walnuts, onions and parsley in a food processor until finely ground.
2. Add all of the other ingredients except the oil and the breadcrumbs.
3. Pulse until well combined and smooth. Check the seasoning.
4. Shape the mixture into 8 small patties with your hands and coat the patties on all sides with bread crumbs.
5. Place in the fridge for 30 minutes to firm.
6. Heat the oil in a skillet over a medium high heat and fry the croquettes until brown on both sides. Serve immediately.

Nutritional Facts per Serving: *Calories 415, Fat 14.1g, Carbs 58.6g, Dietary Fiber 11.3g, Protein 17.1g*

101 Flavorful Plant-Based Recipes For Athletic Performance

COCONUT RICE WITH BLACK BEANS

A delicious combination of coconut and chilies gives this dish a Thai flavor. Try red or yellow bell peppers instead of green. White basmati rice can also be substituted for the brown for an interesting alternative.

Serves 6

INGREDIENTS:

2 teaspoons light vegetable oil

1 finely diced green bell pepper

1 small red onion, finely diced

¼ cup chopped cilantro

1 finely chopped garlic clove

1 teaspoon ground cumin

¼ teaspoon chili powder

3 cups cooked black beans

2 cups coconut milk

2 limes

1½ cups brown basmati rice

½ teaspoon turmeric

4 green spring onions

¼ cup mixed sesame seeds

Salt and pepper to season

Cilantro leaves and pickled onions to garnish

DIRECTIONS:

1. Rinse the rice and put it in a saucepan with 2 cups of water, 1 cup coconut milk and the turmeric. Bring to the boil and simmer until cooked.

Vegan Athlete Cookbook

2. While the rice is cooking heat the oil in a saucepan and add the pepper, red onion and cilantro and cook until tender and the onion is transparent.

3. Add the garlic, cumin, chili, beans and 1 cup coconut milk.

4. Bring to the boil and simmer until hot all the way through.

5. Season with salt and pepper. Squeeze in the juice of one of the limes.

6. When the rice is cooked toss through chopped green spring onions, pepper to taste and the sesame seeds.

7. To serve place the rice on a plate in a nice mound in the center and spoon the bean mixture around it.

8. Garnish with cilantro, pickled onions and the remaining lime cut into wedges.

Nutritional Facts per Serving: *Calories 732, Fat 22.7g, Carbs 108.7g, Dietary Fiber 18.2g, Protein 27.2g*

101 Flavorful Plant-Based Recipes For Athletic Performance

CORN AND BLACK BEAN PATTIES

These contain nutty flavored millet. Leftover patties can be reheated and served with salad for a quick snack. Wow! Now that really gets the taste buds a' tinglin'. Snack on these, or use as part of a more substantial meal.

Make 20

INGREDIENTS:

2 cups millet

2½ cups water

Pure vegetable oil for frying

1 medium onion finely chopped

¼ teaspoon salt

¼ teaspoon chili powder

1 tablespoon powdered paprika

2 teaspoons ground cumin

3 cups cooked black beans – well drained

2 cups fresh sweet corn - cooked

1 cup cornmeal

Freshly ground black pepper

Hot chili sauce to serve

DIRECTIONS:

1. Rinse the millet and drain well.
2. Place a little vegetable oil in a saucepan and add the millet when it is hot. Toss the millet continuously until it is a toasty color and it gives off a nutty aroma.
3. Add the water to the saucepan and cover. Simmer the millet until cooked – about 20 minutes. Drain and set aside to cool a little.

Vegan Athlete Cookbook

4. In a large skillet placed over a medium heat sauté the onion in a little vegetable oil until soft and translucent.

5. Add the salt, chili powder, paprika and cumin stirring well to combine.

6. Add the black beans and the corn and remove from the heat.

7. Add the cooked millet and mash everything together.

8. Season to taste and then add the cornmeal. Mix very well.

9. Heat another skillet over a medium high heat and add 2 tablespoons oil.

10. With damp hands scoop out the bean mixture and form into 2 inch balls. Flatten slightly between your hands and add to the hot oil in the skillet.

11. Fry in batches for 3 – 4 minutes each side until each patty has a nice crisp crust.

12. As the patties are done, remove from the skillet and keep warm until all have been cooked.

13. Serve with hot chili sauce.

Nutritional Facts per Serving: *Calories 148, Fat 1.6g, Carbs 29.5g, Dietary Fiber 5.4g, Protein 5.3g*

101 Flavorful Plant-Based Recipes For Athletic Performance

ALMONDS AND BEANS

A complete protein combination! This is a power packed fully Vegan meal for training athletes – it will get you up and going and keep you sustained.

Serves 4

INGREDIENTS:

2 large tomatoes

2 cups yellow bell peppers, sliced

2 cups broccoli florets

½ teaspoon powdered cumin

½ teaspoon dried basil

½ teaspoon dried marjoram

2 cups kidney beans cooked and drained

3 tablespoons mixed omega oils

1 cup slivered raw almonds

DIRECTIONS:

1. Prepare the vegetables and steam for 30 minutes until tender.
2. Stir through the spice and herbs.
3. Add the kidney beans.
4. Stir through the raw almonds and the omega oils.

Nutritional Facts per Serving: *Calories 730, Fat 37.0g, Carbs 77.5g, Dietary Fiber 23.9g, Protein 35.0g*

Vegan Athlete Cookbook

PUMPKIN SEEDS AND GARBANZO BEANS

Crunchy, delicious pumpkin seeds are high in calories, and they are packed with fibre, vitamins, minerals, and numerous antioxidants. This tastes so good that you will want to cook and serve it at any time of the year.

Serves 4

INGREDIENTS:

2 cups baby spinach

2 tomatoes

2 cups diced yellow summer squash

2 cups cauliflower florets

4 cups cooked garbanzo beans

½ teaspoon turmeric

½ teaspoon dried basil

½ teaspoon dried rosemary

½ cup toasted pumpkin seeds

3 tablespoons mixed omega oils

DIRECTIONS:

1. Prepare the vegetables and steam for 30 minutes until tender.
2. Stir through the spice and herbs.
3. Add garbanzo beans.
4. Stir through the toasted pumpkin seeds and the omega oils.

Nutritional Facts per Serving: *Calories 949, Fat 30.9g, Carbs 132.1g, Dietary Fiber 38.5g, Protein 45.5g*

101 Flavorful Plant-Based Recipes For Athletic Performance

INDIAN BEANS AND RICE

The beans in this recipe are chickpeas and are delicious served with warm naan breads and sliced fresh mango! Add some chopped yellow bell pepper if you desire, or stir some chopped green onions through the rice.

Serves 4

INGREDIENTS:

1 tablespoon curry powder (strength to taste)

½ teaspoon ground cinnamon

1 can chopped tomatoes with chili

2 inch piece of fresh ginger, grated

1 cup brown rice

2 cups cooked chickpeas

1 finely chopped onion

1 finely chopped clove fresh garlic

1 tablespoon vegetable oil

Salt and freshly cracked black pepper

¼ cup chopped cilantro

DIRECTIONS:

1. Rinse the brown rice in water and cook until tender.
2. Heat the oil in a skillet and brown the onions and garlic.
3. Add the chickpeas to the onion mixture. Fry for a minute to heat through properly.
4. Add the curry powder and the cinnamon.
5. Add the tomatoes with their juice and the fresh ginger.
6. Cook on a medium high heat for about 5 minutes until the flavors are well blended.

Vegan Athlete Cookbook

7. When the rice is cooked, remove from the heat and drain. Stir through the chopped cilantro.
8. Serve the beans with the rice.

Nutritional Facts per Serving: *Calories 613, Fat 11.4g, Carbs 106.9g, Dietary Fiber 21.5g, Protein 24.4g*

101 Flavorful Plant-Based Recipes For Athletic Performance

PICCATA NUT AND CHICKPEA MEDALLIONS

A definite Italian twist here! These tasty chickpea cakes can be served with a crunchy salad of lettuce, celery and cucumber for a fully rounded meal.

Serves 4

INGREDIENTS:

1 cup cooked chickpeas

¾ cup roasted unsalted cashew nuts

1 clove garlic, grated

¾ cup wheat flour gluten

2 tablespoon soy sauce

½ teaspoon smoked paprika

¼ teaspoon turmeric powder

2 tablespoons vegetable oil

¼ cup dry white wine

2 tablespoon freshly squeezed lime juice

1 tablespoon chopped capers

2 tablespoons finely chopped parsley

1 tablespoon Vegan margarine

Sea salt and freshly ground black pepper to taste

DIRECTIONS:

1. Pre-heat the oven to 275°F.
2. Place the garlic and cashews in a food processor and process until finely ground.
3. Add the chickpeas and pulse until chopped.
4. Add the flour, sauce, spices and salt to taste.

Vegan Athlete Cookbook

5. Pulse until well mixed.
6. Turn the mixture out into a bowl and mix with your hands to ensure that all of the ingredients are well combined.
7. Divide the mixture into 8 pieces and form each piece into a round flat cake (medallion).
8. In a large skillet heat the vegetable oil. When it is hot add the medallions and cook until nicely browned on both sides – about 10 minutes all together.
9. Place the medallions on a baking sheet and keep them warm while you prepare the sauce.
10. In the same skillet, add the wine, lime juice, capers and parsley and scrap any bits from the base of the pan.
11. Season with salt and pepper and let the liquid simmer until reduce by about a third.
12. Add the margarine to the hot liquid and stir through.
13. Serve the medallions drizzled with the sauce.

Nutritional Facts per Serving: *Calories 525, Fat 25.0g, Carbs 45.0g, Dietary Fiber 9.8g, Protein 31.6g*

101 Flavorful Plant-Based Recipes For Athletic Performance

CRISPY CHICKPEA RISSOLES

Tasty finger food for a party or as a snack for added energy! These rissoles lend themselves to dipping in different sauces.

Serves 6 generously

INGREDIENTS:

2 cups chickpea flour

3 cups water

½ tablespoon sea salt

½ red onion very finely chopped

1 finely grated carrot

1 tablespoon finely chopped fresh rosemary leaves

2 tablespoons olive oil

1 cup dry whole wheat breadcrumbs

Vegetable oil for frying

Vegan tomato sauce for dipping

DIRECTIONS:

1. In a large bowl, whisk together the chickpea flour, water, sea salt, onion, carrot, olive oil and rosemary.
2. Pour into a saucepan set over a medium heat and continue to whisk the mixture until it becomes quite thick.
3. Remove the pan from the heat and continue whisking until there are no lumps in the mixture.
4. Oil a 9 x 12 inch rectangular casserole and spread the chickpea mixture in an even layer onto the base. Leave to cool.
5. Place in the refrigerator for a couple of hours to firm enough to cut into squares.
6. Remove the squares and gently coat in the dried breadcrumbs.

Vegan Athlete Cookbook

7. In a large skillet, pour some of the frying oil to cover the bottom of the pan. Heat the oil until just under smoking point.

8. Fry the rissoles for about 5 minutes, turning half way through this time to ensure that they are brown on both sides.

9. Fry in batches if necessary keeping the finished ones warm while you are doing so.

10. Serve while hot with a dipping sauce.

Nutritional Facts per Serving: *Calories 383, Fat 10.2g, Carbs 59.5g, Dietary Fiber 14.8g, Protein 16.7g*

101 Flavorful Plant-Based Recipes For Athletic Performance

SOUTH SEA ISLAND BEANS AND RICE

So much more than just beans and rice on a plate! Taste the tropical flavors. Add chopped bell peppers, chopped jalapenos or even some toasted coconut to add a delicate nuance!

Serves 4

INGREDIENTS:

1 cup dry brown rice

2 cups cooked beans of your choice

1 finely chopped onion

2 finely chopped cloves garlic

1 tablespoon olive oil

2 cups chopped red cabbage

2 cups fresh baby spinach

2 tablespoons soy sauce

¾ teaspoon Spanish smoked paprika

1 can sliced pineapple, drained and the juice reserved

Salt and pepper to season

DIRECTIONS:

1. Cook the rice in plenty of water with some salt.
2. While the rice is cooking fry the onion and garlic in a skillet with the olive oil. When soft add the beans and heat through.
3. Stir in the red cabbage, ½ cup pineapple juice, 1 tablespoon soy sauce and paprika and cook for about 5 minutes only. The cabbage must remain crunchy.
4. Stir in the baby spinach and cook until it is slightly wilted. Season to taste with salt and pepper.
5. While the vegetables are cooking sauté the pineapple rings in a

Vegan Athlete Cookbook

little oil until golden on both sides. Brush with the remaining 1 tablespoon soy sauce.

6. Serve the beans and rice on a plate and top with the pineapple rings.

Nutritional Facts per Serving: *Calories 385, Fat 5.4g, Carbs 76.2g, Dietary Fiber 10.3g, Protein 15.2g*

101 Flavorful Plant-Based Recipes For Athletic Performance

TUSCAN RAPINI BEANS

The rich dark green of the broccoli rabe (rapini) and the white beans is a feast for the eyes. Serve with rice, pasta or a chunk of freshly baked bread to mop up all of the juices.

Serves 4

INGREDIENTS:

1 medium bunch rapini, washed

2 tablespoons vegetable oil

2 finely chopped cloves garlic

3 cups cooked white beans

1 teaspoon finely chopped rosemary leaves

Salt and freshly ground black pepper to season

DIRECTIONS:

1. Pick over the rapini and remove any thick tough stems.
2. Boil some water in a large sauce pan and add some salt and the rapini. Cook for about 6 minutes until tender.
3. Drain the rapini and run under cold water to keep the color. Drain again and chop coarsely.
4. Heat the veg a medium heat and add the garlic. Cook for about 30 seconds making sure that it does not burn.
5. Stir in the beans, the rosemary and the chopped rapini.
6. Season with salt and pepper and gently cook together for about 8 minutes until piping hot.
7. Serve.

***Nutritional Facts per Serving:** Calories 573, Fat 8.2g, Carbs 92.5g, Dietary Fiber 23.7g, Protein 36.2g*

ADUKI BEANS AND GREENS

Nutty flavors mingle with the sweet, salty and sour of the ume plum vinegar.

Serves 4

INGREDIENTS:

1 cup millet, rinsed and drained

2 cups homemade vegetable stock

2 carrots, thinly sliced

1 cup cooked aduki beans

1 medium bunch collard greens

2 tablespoons olive oil

6 generous drops of ume plum vinegar

¼ cup roasted pumpkin seeds

Salt and pepper to season

DIRECTIONS:

1. Heat a heavy based saucepan to a low heat and stir the millet around in it for 3 – 4 minutes to take on a brown color and a toasty flavor.

2. Add the vegetable stock carefully as it will spit as it hits the hot pan. Bring to the boil.

3. Place the carrots, chopped collard greens and beans on top of the millet as it is cooking. Do not stir them in! Place the lid on the pot and turn the heat up to medium.

4. Cook for about 20 minutes or until all of the vegetable stock has been absorbed.

5. Remove from the heat and stir through the vinegar and olive oil. Top with the pumpkin seeds.

101 Flavorful Plant-Based Recipes For Athletic Performance

Nutritional Facts per Serving: *Calories 354, Fat 11.8g, Carbs 52.8g, Dietary Fiber 9.2g, Protein 11.3g*

BARBEQUED BLACK-EYED PEA ROLLS

Not just your ordinary cabbage roll!

Serves 4

INGREDIENTS:

12 large collard greens leaves

2 cups chopped collard greens

1 tablespoon olive oil

8 ounces cremini or brown mushrooms, sliced

1½ cups cooked black-eyed peas

3 cups barbeque sauce

DIRECTIONS:

1. Boil some water in a large saucepan and add the large collard leaves. Leave to cook for about 5 minutes. Remove the leaves with tongs, drain and let cool. Open them out gently on a board or large tray if you have room.
2. Heat the oil in a large skillet over a medium heat and sauté the mushrooms until soft – about 5 minutes.
3. Add the chopped collard greens to the mushrooms and cook for about 8 minutes until all of the moisture has disappeared. Add the peas and cook through.
4. Pour in 2 cups of barbeque sauce and cook together for another 5 minutes or so until thick and not watery.
5. Place 2 tablespoons of the pea mixture onto each large cooled leaf about third of the way down the leaf. Turn up the bottom over the pea mixture. Turn in each side of the leaf and roll up fairly firmly.
6. Serve with the rest of the sauce poured over the rolls.

Nutritional Facts per Serving: *Calories 400, Fat 5.0g, Carbs 83.6g, Dietary Fiber 5.2g, Protein 6.4g*

101 Flavorful Plant-Based Recipes For Athletic Performance

PINTO AND PLANTAIN STEW

A delicious stew that is served with crispy parsnip chips! So easy and so moreish – enjoy.

Serves 4

INGREDIENTS:

1 tablespoon olive oil

1 large red onion, finely chopped

1 yellow or red bell pepper, seeded and finely chopped

3 hot red chili peppers, seeded and minced

4 cloves finely chopped garlic

2 tins plum tomatoes

¼ cup vegetable stock

½ teaspoon sea salt

2 teaspoons powdered cumin

1 x 15 ounce can pinto beans

2 ripe plantains, peeled and halved lengthwise

1½ cups unsweetened shredded coconut

1 cup chopped cilantro

1 pound parsnips

1 tablespoon peanut oil

DIRECTIONS:

1. In a saucepan over a medium heat, fry the onion, pepper, chili and garlic for about 6 minutes until soft.

2. Add tomatoes, stock, salt and cumin. Cover with a lid and let simmer for about 12 minutes. Stir occasionally until the tomatoes have pulped.

Vegan Athlete Cookbook

3. Add the beans and the plantains which have been cut into half inch pieces.
4. Cover and simmer for another 20 minutes until the plantains are soft.
5. Add the cilantro and mix in.
6. While the bean mixture is cooking make the parsnip chips.
7. Preheat the oven to 400°F.
8. Prepare a baking sheet and cover with parchment paper.
9. Peel the parsnips and slice thinly.
10. Lay the parsnip slices on the baking sheet and drizzle with oil.
11. Bake in the hot oven for 15 minutes.
12. Turn the chips over and bake for another 10 – 15 minutes. Drizzle over a little more oil if necessary.
13. When the chips are crisp remove from the oven and sprinkle with salt.
14. Serve the beans in bowls topped with the parsnip chips.

Nutritional Facts per Serving: *Calories 938, Fat 33.3g, Carbs 133.1g, Dietary Fiber 32.3g, Protein 30.0g*

101 Flavorful Plant-Based Recipes For Athletic Performance

SOUPS

GINGER SOUP

A cold tangy soup which is just right for a warm summer's day! Use ice cold water for a colder drink.

Serves 4

INGREDIENTS:

7 large carrots

½ ripe avocado

Grated fresh ginger to taste

Salt to taste

Water as required

DIRECTIONS:

1. Scoop the avocado flesh into a blender.
2. Clean and grate the carrots into the blender.
3. Add a half a cup of water to begin with.
4. Whizz the mixture for a few seconds. Add salt and grated ginger to taste.
5. Blend some more and taste again. Adjust salt and ginger as necessary. Add more water for a thinner consistency
6. Serve in glasses

Nutritional Facts per Serving: *Calories 101, Fat 5.2g, Carbs 12.2g, Dietary Fiber 5.2g, Protein 1.6g*

101 Flavorful Plant-Based Recipes For Athletic Performance

CARROT AND GINGER SOUP

A delicious vegetable soup which is best served lukewarm! Flavorful and utterly repeatable!

Serves 4

INGREDIENTS:

10 large carrots

2 hearts of celery

4 tomatoes

2 red bell peppers

3 inch piece fresh ginger root

½ small shallot

½ cup coconut water

4 tablespoons fresh lime juice

1 teaspoon cumin

1 teaspoon curry powder

1 teaspoon salt

Pinch cayenne pepper

Extra virgin olive oil to serve

DIRECTIONS:

1. Blend together all of the vegetables.
2. Add the spices to taste.
3. Warm the soup in a saucepan until just warm.
4. Add the coconut water and lime juice.
5. Serve in glasses with a little olive oil drizzled on the top.

Nutritional Facts per Serving: *Calories 152, Fat 3.5g, Carbs 28.6g, Dietary Fiber 9.1g, Protein 3.6g*

Vegan Athlete Cookbook

BUTTERNUT APPLE SOUP

Another soup to serve lukewarm, with apples and butternut as the core ingredients! This soup has a delicate sweet flavor!

Serves 4

INGREDIENTS:

1 peeled and seeded large butternut squash

2 large green apples, cored

2 large carrots, grated

½ small red onion

1 cup coconut water

1 teaspoon sea salt

½ teaspoon ground cinnamon

½ teaspoon freshly ground nutmeg

Extra virgin olive oil to serve

DIRECTIONS:

1. Place all of the vegetables and the apple in a blender and blend until smooth.
2. Pour into a saucepan and warm through.
3. Add the flavorings and the coconut water.
4. Taste for seasoning.
5. Serve in glasses with the olive oil drizzled on top.

Nutritional Facts per Serving: *Calories 223, Fat 2.9g, Carbs 51.5g, Dietary Fiber 9.7g, Protein 3.4g*

101 Flavorful Plant-Based Recipes For Athletic Performance

HOT AND SOUR MUSHROOM SOUP

This soup has a distinctive Asian flavor with pieces of mushroom and tofu. It is quite filling and could be served as a main meal. Try with warm, crusty bread straight from the oven!

Serves 4

INGREDIENTS:

½ ounce dried wood ear mushrooms

2 cups boiling water

8 cabbage leaves

4 cups homemade vegetable stock

¼ each of soy sauce and rice vinegar

3 tablespoons hot chili oil

½ teaspoon sesame oil

1 teaspoon freshly ground white pepper

1¼ cups sliced fresh mushrooms

1 tablespoon corn-starch

1 cup cold water

1 pound extra firm tofu pressed and cut into matchstick sized pieces

¼ cup shredded carrot

Cup chopped green onions

DIRECTIONS:

1. Reconstitute the wood ear mushrooms by covering them with the boiling water and leaving aside for 20 minutes. Drain.
2. Finely slice the cabbage leaves and set aside.
3. In a large saucepan, pour the stock, soy sauce, rice vinegar, chili oil, sesame oil and white pepper. Cover and bring to the boil.

4. When the stock mixture is boiling, add the cabbage and fresh mushrooms. Cook until the cabbage has wilted – about 6 minutes.

5. Cut the wood ears into small pieces and add to the soup.

6. Mix the corn-starch with the cold water until dissolved and then add to the hot soup, stirring continuously until slightly thickened.

7. Add the carrots and tofu sticks and cook until just heated through.

8. Ladle into bowls. Garnish with the chopped green onions.

Nutritional Facts per Serving: *Calories 222, Fat 15.9g, Carbs 11.6g, Dietary Fiber 4.1g, Protein 12.0g*

101 Flavorful Plant-Based Recipes For Athletic Performance

SUMMER CURRY SOUP

As sunny as a summer's day! Now sit back and wait for the compliments.

Serves 4

INGREDIENTS:

3 x 15 ounce cans coconut milk

¼ cup lemon juice

Juice of 1 fresh lime

½ cup olive oil

½ cup soy sauce

1½ tablespoons Tandoori curry powder

3 inch piece fresh ginger

4 cloves fresh garlic

Salt to taste

Cherry tomatoes, shitake mushrooms and chopped fresh mint to serve

DIRECTIONS:

1. Combine all of the ingredients except the coconut milk, tomatoes, shitake mushrooms and the mint in a blender and blend until well combined.
2. Add the coconut milk and blend again
3. Pour into bowls. Scoop off any foam that may have formed and garnish with the tomatoes, mushrooms and fresh mint.

Nutritional Facts per Serving: *Calories 994, Fat 101.7g, Carbs 26.5g, Dietary Fiber 9.3g, Protein 10.4g*

CORN CHOWDER

This makes a large pot of delicious soup which will certainly warm you on a winter's day! Enjoy in front of the fire with friends and family.

Serves 8

INGREDIENTS:

8 small potatoes, peeled and cut into half inch cubes

¼ teaspoon sea salt

¼ cup olive oil

1 large onion diced

1 clove finely chopped garlic

3 large stalks celery, diced

1 large carrot, diced

½ teaspoon ground cumin

¼ teaspoon cayenne pepper

3 tablespoons flour

2 quarts warm vegetable stock

1 tablespoon vegetable oil

1 large red bell pepper cut into dice

1 large yellow bell pepper cut into dice

1 large green pepper cut into dice

4 cups frozen corn kernels

1 teaspoon salt

½ teaspoon white pepper

3 tablespoons chopped fresh cilantro

Diced tomatoes to garnish

101 Flavorful Plant-Based Recipes For Athletic Performance

DIRECTIONS:

1. Place the potatoes in a small pot. Add the sea salt, cover with water and bring to the boil. Boil until the potatoes are tender – about 3 minutes. Drain and cool.

2. In a large saucepan over a medium heat add the olive oil and sauté the onions, garlic, celery, carrots and spices until soft – about 8 minutes.

3. Add the flour to the pot and stir well so that lumps do not form. Cook for a couple of minutes so that the floury taste disappears.

4. Remove the pot from the heat and slowly add the warm vegetable stock, stirring all the while so the mixture is smooth and no lumps form.

5. When the mixture is smooth return to the heat. Bring to the boil, stirring occasionally so that the bottom does not burn. Cook for about 12 minutes until the soup thickens.

6. While the soup is cooking add the vegetable oil to a skillet and heat over a medium high heat. Add all of the peppers and sauté until tender.

7. Add the corn, peppers and the potatoes to the soup. Season with salt and pepper and the chopped cilantro.

8. Taste and adjust seasoning if necessary.

9. Serve in large warmed bowls and garnish with chopped tomatoes.

Nutritional Facts per Serving: *Calories 307, Fat 9.2g, Carbs 53.1g, Dietary Fiber 9.2g, Protein 7.1g*

Vegan Athlete Cookbook

THAI LEMONGRASS SOUP

Easy to make and flexible in terms of ingredients! Make this for lunch or for dinner. Try broccoli instead of the bok choy and perhaps a different type of mushroom such as oyster mushrooms.

Serves 4

INGREDIENTS:

6 cups tasty homemade vegetable stock

2 stalks lemon grass

3 whole kaffir lime leaves

1½ cups soft tofu

½ teaspoon dried crushed chili

4 garlic cloves, minced

1 2 inch piece fresh ginger or galangal, cut into matchstick pieces

1 cup shitake mushrooms

2 cups baby bok choy

1 cup cherry tomatoes

½ can coconut cream

1 teaspoon brown sugar

4 tablespoons soy sauce

1 tablespoon freshly squeezed lime juice

½ cup fresh basil torn and ¼ cup chopped cilantro roughly chopped

DIRECTIONS:

1. Pour the stock into a large saucepan. Bruise the lemon grass and add to the pot together with the lime leaves, chili, garlic and galangal or ginger. Bring to the boil and boil for 5 minutes.

101 Flavorful Plant-Based Recipes For Athletic Performance

2. Add the shitake mushrooms and simmer for about 5 minutes over a lower heat.

3. Add the bok choy and cherry tomatoes. Simmer for another minute.

4. Reduce the heat to low and add the coconut milk, sugar, soy sauce and lime juice.

5. Finally add the tofu.

6. Taste and add more chili in you like, soy sauce or sugar to give a pleasant sweet/sour flavor.

7. Serve ladled into bowls and garnish with basil and cilantro.

Nutritional Facts per Serving: *Calories 177, Fat 8.7g, Carbs 17.8g, Dietary Fiber 4.4g, Protein 10.8g*

CHILI LENTIL SOUP WITH PINEAPPLE

Definitely try this one! It's easy, yet unique.

Serves 6

INGREDIENTS:

1 tablespoon chili powder (to taste)

2 tablespoons olive oil

1 large red onion, diced

2 finely chopped cloves garlic

2 bay leaves

1 teaspoon sea salt

2 cups washed green lentils

8 cups homemade vegetable stock

2 tablespoons lime juice

6 pineapple rings

Slices of lime

Hot chili sauce

DIRECTIONS:

1. Pre-heat a large saucepan over a medium heat and add the olive oil.
2. Sauté the onion in the oil until soft. Add the garlic and cook for another minute making sure that it does not burn.
3. Add the chili powder and mix it into the onions.
4. Add the bay leaves, lentils, salt and the water and mix well.
5. Bring the soup to the boil and then reduce the heat and simmer for about half an hour, stirring a couple of times.
6. Hear a grill pan and oil lightly. Grill the pineapple rings for 4

minutes on each side until grill lines appear.

7. Once the lentils are tender, thin the soup with some extra water if it is too thick. Add the lime juice and stir well.

8. Remove the bay leaf and puree half of the soup to give a thicker texture.

9. Taste and season with salt if necessary.

10. Ladle into bowls and top with a pineapple ring, slices of lime and a few drops of chili sauce.

Nutritional Facts per Serving: *Calories 318, Fat 5.9g, Carbs 49.4g, Dietary Fiber 22.3g, Protein 18.4g*

Vegan Athlete Cookbook

BURGERS & NOT-MEAT MEALS

101 Flavorful Plant-Based Recipes For Athletic Performance

ALMOND AND FLAXSEED BURGERS

A raw burger which is very filling! Serve with salad on the side. Add extra garlic if you like the taste.

Serves 4

INGREDIENTS:

2 cup raw almonds

1 cup ground flaxseed

2 cloves garlic

4 tablespoons balsamic vinegar

4 tablespoons hemp oil

Sea salt

DIRECTIONS:

1. Place all of the ingredients into a blender and pulse until well blended. Add salt to taste.
2. Form into 4 patties

Nutritional Facts per Serving: Calories 586, Fat 49.4g, Carbs 10.9g, Dietary Fiber 20.8g, Protein 21.3g

Vegan Athlete Cookbook

VEGGIE BURGERS

These smoky burgers are packed full of all of the good things! Serve while still warm with vegetables or a side salad.

Serves 4

INGREDIENTS:

8 ounces dried lentils

3 cups water

1 large onion, diced

2 tablespoons vegetable oil

3 portabella mushrooms

3 cloves garlic minced

1½ teaspoons salt and pepper

2 tablespoons tomato paste

½ teaspoon thyme

½ cup red wine

2 teaspoons balsamic vinegar

2 tablespoons Vegan Worcestershire sauce

1 teaspoon liquid smoke

1 cup chopped pecans

¾ cup ground flaxseed

¾ cup wheat gluten

DIRECTIONS:

1. Wash the lentils and cook in the water until tender – about half an hour.
2. Fry the onion in the oil until soft. Add the mushrooms and garlic and fry until soft.

101 Flavorful Plant-Based Recipes For Athletic Performance

3. Stir in the tomato paste, salt, thyme and pepper. Stir in the chopped pecans and fry until toasty.
4. Add the wine, vinegar, sauce and liquid smoke. Stir in the cooked lentils.
5. Remove the pan from the heat and add the flaxseed and wheat gluten. Stir continuously to develop the gluten and allow the mixture to become chewy.
6. Form into 8 patties and place in the fridge for an hour to cool.
7. Meanwhile pre-heat the oven to 350°F.
8. Sprinkle a baking tray with cornmeal.
9. Arrange the patties on the baking tray and bake in the hot oven for 30 minutes. Turn the patties halfway through the cooking time.

Nutritional Facts per Serving: Calories 677, Fat 27.6g, Carbs 54.9g, Dietary Fiber 21.3g, Protein 50.7g

VEGAN BACON

A smoky soy flavored dish with hint of maple syrup. Delicious for breakfast or as a filling in a toasty.

Serves 4

INGREDIENTS:

½ cup dried small red beans of your choice

1/3 cup hulled wholegrain buckwheat

1 teaspoon onion powder

1 teaspoon hickory liquid smoke

4 teaspoons nutritional yeast

1 tablespoon soy sauce

½ teaspoon sea salt

3 teaspoons tomato paste

1 teaspoon coconut oil

2 teaspoon maple syrup

DIRECTIONS:

1. Rinse the beans and the buckwheat and soak overnight in a bowl of water.
2. The next morning pre-heat the oven to 400°F.
3. Line a 9 x 13 pan with parchment paper and oil lightly.
4. Rinse the beans and the buckwheat and drain well.
5. Place in a processor together with the other ingredients.
6. Pulse to combine until a uniform but not puree texture is formed.
7. Place the mixture in the baking pan and spread very thinly with a spatula.

101 Flavorful Plant-Based Recipes For Athletic Performance

8. Bake for 10 minutes in the hot oven. Remove and let cool for 10 minutes.

9. Slice into 24 strips and remove the strips from the pan with a small spatula.

10. Heat a tablespoon of oil on a high heat in a skillet.

11. Fry the bacon slices for 3 minutes, flipping half way through the cooking time.

12. Serve.

Nutritional Facts per Serving: Calories 164, Fat 2.1g, Carbs 29.5g, Dietary Fiber 6.0g, Protein 9.1g

Vegan Athlete Cookbook

BEAN AND BEET BURGERS

Sunday morning Brunch! Try serving with maple syrup.

Makes 6

INGREDIENTS:

1 pound red beets

½ cup raw brown rice

1 onion, diced small

3 cloves garlic, minced

2 tablespoons apple cider vinegar

¼ cup rolled oats

2 x 15 oz. cans black beans

¼ cup prunes, chopped small

1 tablespoon extra-virgin olive oil

1 tablespoon smoked paprika

2 teaspoons brown mustard

1 teaspoon cumin

½ teaspoon coriander

½ teaspoon dried thyme

Salt and pepper

DIRECTIONS:

1. Pre-heat the oven to 400°F.
2. Wrap beets loosely in foil and roast until easily pierced with a fork, 50 to 60 minutes. Set aside to cool.
3. Meanwhile, bring a large pot of water to a boil. Salt water generously and add rice. Simmer for about 30 minutes. Drain and set it aside to cool.

101 Flavorful Plant-Based Recipes For Athletic Performance

4. Heat a teaspoon of olive oil in a skillet over medium-high heat. Add the onions and a pinch of salt and cook until golden. About 10 minutes.

5. Add the garlic and cook for 30 seconds.

6. Pour in the vinegar and scrape up the dark sticky crust from under the onions. Simmer until cider has evaporated and the pan is nearly dry. Remove from heat and set aside.

7. Place the oats in a food processor and process until they have reduced to a fine flour. Transfer to a small bowl and set aside.

8. Drain and rinse one of the cans of beans and place in the food processor. Scatter the prunes on top. Pulse until chopped.

9. Transfer this mixture to a large mixing bowl. Drain and rinse the second can of beans and add to the bowl.

10. Peel the beets and grate them coarsely. Squeeze them to remove any extra liquid.

11. Put the squeezed beets, cooked rice, and sautéed onions into the bowl with the beans. Sprinkle olive oil, mustard, paprika, cumin, coriander, and thyme over the mixture. Mix until combined.

12. Season to taste with salt and pepper.

13. Refrigerate the mixture for a couple of hours.

14. When ready to cook, first shape the mixture into 6 patties.

15. Fry in a skillet over a high heat for a couple of minutes on each side. Cover the pan and cook gently until heated right through – about 4 minutes.

16. Serve the veggie burgers on burger buns or lightly toasted sandwich bread along with some fresh greens.

Nutritional Facts per Serving: *Calories 639, Fat 5.4g, Carbs 117.9g, Dietary Fiber 25.3g, Protein 34.2g*

PORTABELLO MUSHROOM BURGERS

Mushrooms and caramelized onions! Heady kitchen aromas. Add Dijon mustard on top of the onions for a taste bud tingle!

Makes 8

INGREDIENTS:

8 Portobello mushroom caps

1 tablespoon finely chopped fresh rosemary

½ cup soy sauce

4 cups water

4 tablespoons olive oil

4 white or yellow onions, thinly sliced into rings

1 tablespoon balsamic vinegar

5 cups salad rocket

Tomato and avocado slices

Whole wheat burger buns

DIRECTIONS:

1. Wipe the mushroom caps and remove the stems.
2. Marinate the mushrooms in a mixture of the soy sauce, water and rosemary for at least 2 hours.
3. When the mushrooms have finished marinading, heat a skillet over a medium heat and add the olive oil.
4. Add the onion slices to the hot pan and sauté them until they become soft and translucent. Add the balsamic vinegar to the onions and continue to cook until the onions are soft and most of the liquid has evaporated.
5. Drain the mushroom caps and grill them under a hot grill for about 10 minutes until soft.

6. Halve the buns and toast. Place a mushroom cap on the bottom of each and top it with caramelized onions.
7. Place the rocket and avocado slices on top.
8. Top with the other piece of bun.
9. Serve.

Nutritional Facts per Serving: *Calories 309, Fat 15.5g, Carbs 35.4g, Dietary Fiber 3.1g, Protein 9.6g*

BROCCOLI 'BEEF' WITH QUINOA

A superb high protein dinner to share! Add some extra soy and chili sauce if desired.

Serves 4

INGREDIENTS:

1¼ cups dry quinoa

1½ cups water

1 pound wheat gluten

2 cloves garlic, finely chopped

1 red onion, diced

1 large head fresh broccoli, cut into pieces

1 tablespoon vegetable oil

1 tablespoon corn-starch

1 teaspoon maple syrup

½ teaspoon finely chopped red chili

2 teaspoons fresh ginger, minced

1 tablespoon black bean paste

¼ cup white wine

½ cup vegetable stock

2 tablespoons fresh orange juice

1 tablespoon light soy sauce

DIRECTIONS:

1. Bring the water to a boil, add quinoa and reduce heat to medium-low. Let simmer for 12 minutes until tender, let stand 5 minutes. Fluff with fork when ready to serve.

2. Combine the cornstarch, maple syrup, chopped chili, ginger,

bean paste, wine, stock, orange juice and soy sauce in a bowl and mix well to dissolve corn starch. Set aside.

3. Heat the two teaspoons vegetable oil in a large skillet over medium-high heat. Add the wheat gluten, stirring occasionally for 2-3 minutes to brown. Transfer to a plate and set aside.

4. Heat the remaining oil in the same pan over medium-high heat. Add the onion and garlic; cook for two minutes and add broccoli. Cover and let cook for 5-10 minutes. When the broccoli is tender but still a little crisp add sauce and browned wheat gluten and cook until the sauce thickens slightly.

5. Serve.

Nutritional Facts per Serving: *Calories 734, Fat 8.5g, Carbs 67.3g, Dietary Fiber 5.4g, Protein 96.0g*

Vegan Athlete Cookbook

WRAPS & SANDWICHES

101 Flavorful Plant-Based Recipes For Athletic Performance

EGGPLANT AND HOISIN OPEN SANDWICHES

An amazing combination of flavors in a very special sandwich! Yum! Use different breads or even a toasted bun.

Serves 4

INGREDIENTS:

1 medium eggplant

3 tablespoons vegetable oil

2 teaspoons toasted sesame oil

¼ teaspoon salt

1 cup tomato purée

¼ cup hoisin sauce

1 tablespoon agave nectar

8 ounces wheat gluten, cut into finger thick slices

4 large slices of your favorite bread

8 green onions, thinly sliced

1 tablespoon sesame seeds

DIRECTIONS:

1. Pre-heat the oven to 425°F. Place a baking pan in the oven to get hot. Turn on the grill to high.
2. Cut the eggplant into 4 thick slices lengthwise. Cut off the layer of skin on the outer 2 slices.
3. Brush the eggplant with a combination of 2 tablespoons vegetable oil and 1 teaspoon of the sesame oil. Sprinkle with salt and put on the hot grill for about 5 minutes each side until nicely toasted.
4. Transfer to the hot baking pan in the oven to keep warm.
5. To make the sauce mix together the tomato purée, hoisin

sauce, agave nectar and the remaining teaspoon of sesame oil in a small saucepan over a medium heat.

6. Toss the wheat gluten fingers in the remaining vegetable oil. Place on the grill and grill each side for about 3 minutes each.

7. Add the gluten to the sauce in the pan. Stir well and reduce the heat to keep it hot but not bubbling.

8. Toast the bread slices. Put a piece of eggplant on each and put on plates.

9. Top each slice with the hot sauce. Sprinkle with the chopped onions and the sesame seeds.

Nutritional Facts per Serving: *Calories 492, Fat 15.7g, Carbs 42.6g, Dietary Fiber 7.0g, Protein 47.7g*

101 Flavorful Plant-Based Recipes For Athletic Performance

GRILLED ONION AND EGGPLANT BREAD ROLLS

The versatile eggplant is again the star of these tasty morsels! Simple, sensational and utterly delicious.

Serves 4

INGREDIENTS:

4 x 1 inch thick eggplant slices

1 large red onion cut into 4 thick slices

4 large tomato slices

Lettuce leaves

4 whole wheat buns

Garlic salt and black pepper

¾ cup of your favorite grilling marinade

DIRECTIONS:

1. Soak 4 wooden skewers for about 15 minutes in water.
2. Push a skewer through each onion slice to keep the rings together.
3. Marinate the onions and eggplant in the marinade of choice for about 20 minutes.
4. Pre-heat a grill.
5. Remove the vegetables from the marinade and grill for 15 to 20 minutes.
6. Towards the end of the cooking time, toast the buns.
8. Serve the buns open on a plate with the vegetables on top. Sprinkle with garlic salt and pepper. Top with crisp lettuce leaves.

Nutritional Facts per Serving: *Calories 246, Fat 4.8g, Carbs 45.6g, Dietary Fiber 6.9g, Protein 7.7g*

Vegan Athlete Cookbook

SAUCY WHEATBALL SUBS

Plenty for everyone with a tangy sauce! These are delicious and the recipe should leave you with enough for leftovers.

Makes 28

INGREDIENTS:

1½ cups cooked chickpeas

1 cup chopped brown mushrooms

3 minced cloves garlic

2 tablespoons freshly minced parsley

2 tablespoons tomato paste

2 tablespoon soy sauce

1 tablespoon water

2½ tablespoons vegetable oil plus extra for cooking

½ cup dry breadcrumbs

½ cup wheat gluten flour

¾ cup nutritional yeast

2 teaspoons dried mixed herbs

½ teaspoon paprika

Salt and pepper to taste

3 tablespoons corn starch

½ teaspoon garlic powder

2 cups unsweetened soy milk

2 teaspoons fresh lime juice

2 teaspoons apple cider vinegar

1 teaspoon English mustard

2 cups Marinara sauce

101 Flavorful Plant-Based Recipes For Athletic Performance

4 sub rolls

DIRECTIONS:

1. In a food processor, combine the chickpeas, mushrooms, garlic, and parsley. Pulse until coarsely ground.

2. Add the tomato paste, soy sauce, water, oil, breadcrumbs, gluten flour, ¼ cup of the yeast, herbs, paprika and salt and pepper to taste. Pulse to combine.

3. Scrape the mixture into a large bowl and knead with slightly damp hands until well blended. Pinch off piece and roll into golf ball sized balls.

4. Heat a thin layer of oil in a large skillet and fry the balls in batches until brown all over, turning when necessary. This will take about 5 minutes. There will be some extras and these can be stored in the fridge.

5. In a medium saucepan, combine the rest of the yeast, cornstarch, and soy and garlic powder. Over a medium heat whisk in the soy milk.

6. Stir and cook for about a minute until the sauce thickens. Remove from the heat. Stir in 1 tablespoon oil, the lime juice, vinegar and mustard.

7. In a large saucepan combine 16 of the wheat balls and the Marinara sauce and heat through. Mash a few of the wheat balls but most must retain their shape.

8. Split the sub rolls lengthways and toast them. Arrange on plates to serve.

9. Divide the wheat ball mixture among the subs and top with the sauce.

10. Serve hot!

Nutritional Facts per Serving: *Calories 148, Fat 3.4g, Carbs 23.6g, Dietary Fiber 4.3g, Protein 7.1g*

Vegan Athlete Cookbook

CELERIAC WRAPS

Fresh vegetable goodness in a parcel!

Serves 4

INGREDIENTS:

2 crisp carrots

2 large celeriac roots

2 medium green apples

1 small avocado

2 tablespoons chopped parsley

4 large wraps

Sweet red or yellow pepper, chopped

Sliced tomato, sliced cucumber

Lettuce leaves

DIRECTIONS:

1. Chop the celeriac, carrot and apple and blend together. Add chopped parsley and the avocado which has been mashed.
2. Warm the wraps to make them more pliable and fill each with 4 tablespoons of the celeriac mix, some pepper, lettuce, sliced tomato and cucumber.
3. Serve.

Nutritional Facts per Serving: *Calories 352, Fat 13.2g, Carbs 51.7g, Dietary Fiber 9.3g, Protein 5.7g*

101 Flavorful Plant-Based Recipes For Athletic Performance

SALADS, VEGGIES & SIDES

Vegan Athlete Cookbook

CELERY AND BEETROOT SALAD

A delicious salad with a tangy lemon dressing! This salad does not keep and it needs to be eaten as soon as it is made however with a flavor combo like this, that shouldn't be a problem.

Serves 6

INGREDIENTS:

1 bunch arugula (salad rocket)

1 bunch watercress

1 large cooked beetroot

1 small celery root

1 green apple

1 small red onion

1/3 cup freshly squeezed lemon juice

2 tablespoons roasted garlic purée

1 tablespoon Dijon mustard

1 tablespoon maple syrup

¼ cup extra virgin olive oil

¼ cup flax oil

½ cup coarsely chopped pecans

Salt and pepper to taste

DIRECTIONS:

1. Wash the arugula and watercress and remove any coarse stems. Allow to soak in cold water while preparing the rest of the salad.

2. Peel the beetroot, celery and apple and cut each one into this julienne strips or grate them coarsely on a grater.

3. Cut the onion into this slices

101 Flavorful Plant-Based Recipes For Athletic Performance

4. Combine all of the remaining ingredients, except for the pecans, and whisk together in a large bowl until emulsified.
5. Add the vegetable strips and toss until well coated. Leave for a few minutes for the flavors to combine.
6. Drain the greens and pat gently to dry or use a salad spinner.
7. Add the vegetables and toss everything well together.
8. Sprinkle the walnuts on top and serve.

Nutritional Facts per Serving: *Calories 267, Fat 25.3g, Carbs 11.4g, Dietary Fiber 2.5g, Protein 1.9g*

Vegan Athlete Cookbook

FRESH KALE AND CRANBERRY SALAD

Make this one the night before! The kale will become less tough if stored overnight in the fridge. Add different nuts if you don't have pine nuts and the lime juice may be substituted by lemon juice

Serves 4

INGREDIENTS:

1 bunch fresh kale, well washed, dried and finely chopped

1 small red onion, thinly sliced

1 stalk celery, washed and thinly sliced

½ ripe avocado cubed

¼ cup dried cranberries

Toasted pine nuts

½ cup cooked, drained chickpeas

Lime juice and olive oil to taste

Sea salt and freshly grated black pepper

DIRECTIONS:

1. Mix all of the ingredients together in a large bowl.
2. Serve immediately or store in the refrigerator until required.

Nutritional Facts per Serving: *Calories 192, Fat 10.4g, Carbs 19.5g, Dietary Fiber 7.1g, Protein 6.2g*

101 Flavorful Plant-Based Recipes For Athletic Performance

CHILI CORN SALAD WITH BEANS AND TOMATOES

This is a great side salad or starter. Double quantities if you would like to serve as a main. Smoked paprika gives this salad a special flavor. Enjoy.

Serves 4

INGREDIENTS:

2 cups fresh corn kernels

1½ cups cooked white lima beans

8 ounces small red cherry tomatoes

1 small red onion, sliced thinly

2 tablespoons finely chopped cilantro

3 tablespoons lime juice

1 teaspoon hot smoked paprika

2 tablespoons extra virgin olive oil

2 teaspoon agave nectar

1 teaspoon dried marjoram

Salt and freshly ground pepper to taste

DIRECTIONS:

1. Cook the corn kernels in a large pot of boiling water until cooked but still crunchy. Drain well and set aside to cool.
2. Place the corn in a large bowl and add the beans.
3. Halve the tomatoes and add to the corn, together with the onion and cilantro.
4. Whisk together the rest of the ingredients and season as desired. Pour over the corn mix.
5. Cover and chill for half an hour before serving.

Nutritional Facts per Serving: *Calories 232, Fat 8.2g, Carbs 37.8g, Dietary Fiber 6.4g, Protein 6.9g*

Vegan Athlete Cookbook

COUSCOUS SALAD WITH DRIED FRUITS AND EDAMAME

Try this for a surprisingly refreshing flavor!

Serves 4

INGREDIENTS:

1 tablespoon olive oil

1 cup uncooked couscous (not instant)

2 cups water

1 cup cooked shelled edamame

1 red bell pepper, diced

½ cup chopped cilantro

½ large red onion, very finely chopped

½ cup dried, ready to eat apricots, chopped

1 cup dried cranberries

1 tablespoon curry powder (strength as you fancy)

1 teaspoon sea salt

Juice of half a lemon

DIRECTIONS:

1. Heat a saucepan over a medium heat. Add the oil and the couscous and toast for a few minutes, stirring constantly so that it does not burn.
2. Add the water and bring to the boil. Cover and simmer for about 12 minutes until soft and the water has been absorbed.
3. In a large bowl stir together the couscous and all of the other ingredients. Let chill in the fridge for about an hour to let the flavors mingle.

Nutritional Facts per Serving: *Calories 280, Fat 6.1g, Carbs 46.4g, Dietary Fiber 6.3g, Protein 10.3g*

CRANBERRY AND NUT SALAD

Fruit and nuts with apple cider vinaigrette! Eat straight away while fresh and crunchy.

Serves 4

INGREDIENTS:

1 green fresh crisp lettuce

1 thinly sliced fennel bulb

1 ripe avocado diced

½ cup dried cranberries

¼ cup chopped macadamia nuts

½ small shallot, diced finely

¼ cup olive oil

3 tablespoons apple cider vinegar

¼ teaspoon Vegan sugar

Salt and pepper to taste

DIRECTIONS:

1. Combine the torn or shredded lettuce in a bowl with the fennel, cranberries and nuts.
2. Blend together the shallot, oil, vinegar, sugar, and seasonings.
3. Pour the dressing over the salad and serve immediately.

Nutritional Facts per Serving: *Calories 307, Fat 29.0g, Carbs 10.5g, Dietary Fiber 7.7g, Protein 3.3g*

Vegan Athlete Cookbook

CURRIED CUCUMBER AND MANGO SALAD

The mango sauce just makes this salad so special! Tropical, summery flavors. Such a simple recipe can taste sensational!

Serves 4

INGREDIENTS:

4 cups cucumber, chopped and de-seeded

1 cup chopped celery

1 fresh mango, skinned, pitted and sliced

1 teaspoon curry powder

Chopped chives

DIRECTIONS:

1. Mix together the cucumber and celery.
2. Mash the mango flesh and mix in the curry powder.
3. Mix the mango sauce into the salad vegetables.
4. Serve

Nutritional Facts per Serving: *Calories 56, Fat 0.5g, Carbs 13.7g, Dietary Fiber 2.2g, Protein 1.2g*

101 Flavorful Plant-Based Recipes For Athletic Performance

CABBAGE AND NECTARINE CHINESE SALAD

Chinese, but also a taste of the South Sea Islands! This is a summer salad to eat when nectarines are in season but you could of course add a different fruit if you so wished.

Serves 4 generously

INGREDIENTS:

4 cups lightly packed finely shredded Chinese cabbage

1 cup finely chopped red onion

1 small fresh pineapple thinly sliced and cut into small pieces

½ teaspoon garlic flavored hot sauce

1 nectarine finely sliced

Olive oil to drizzle

¾ cup chopped macadamias

Salt and pepper to taste

DIRECTIONS:

1. In a large salad bowl, toss together the cabbage and the onion.
2. Place in the fridge to keep cool.
3. In a separate bowl combine the pineapple and the hot sauce. Crush the pineapple to make enough juice to cover the pieces.
4. Place the cabbage and onion on a plate. Top with the pineapple and the sliced nectarine. Drizzle with oil and top with the chopped nuts.
5. Season as required.
6. Do not combine the different parts of the salad until ready to eat as it will go soggy!

Nutritional Facts per Serving: *Calories 347, Fat 26.1g, Carbs 30.5g, Dietary Fiber 5.3g, Protein 4.7g*

Vegan Athlete Cookbook

SUMMER SQUASH AND PASTA SALAD

Everyone loves a pasta salad – it's a complete meal in a bowl! Colorful and reminiscent of Italy with reds, greens and white!

Serves 6

INGREDIENTS:

8 ounces orzo (short-cut pasta)

1 teaspoon salt

3 tablespoons extra-virgin olive oil

2 yellow crookneck squash, trimmed, diced

2 zucchini, trimmed, diced

½ large red onion, diced finely

1 red bell pepper, cored, seeded, diced

1 cup red cherry tomatoes, halved

zest of 1 lemon

2 tablespoons lemon juice

2 teaspoons salt

Freshly ground black pepper

1 tablespoon chopped fresh parsley

4 cups baby spinach

½ cup un-pitted olives

DIRECTIONS:

1. Cook the pasta in plenty of salted boiling water until al dente. Drain and toss with 1 teaspoon of oil. Set aside.

2. In a large bowl gently mix together the squash, zucchini, onion, tomatoes and bell pepper.

3. In a small bowl combine the oil, juice, zest, salt and pepper to

taste and the parsley and stir well together.

4. Pour over the vegetables and toss. Add the pasta and once more check for seasoning.
5. Divide the spinach up among 6 plates. Top with the pasta mixture.
6. Serve with olives on the side.

Nutritional Facts per Serving: *Calories 270, Fat 11.2g, Carbs 35.4g, Dietary Fiber 3.9g, Protein 7.2g*

Vegan Athlete Cookbook

ZUCCHINI PASTA SALAD

Ok, I lied - there is no pasta in this one, just an amazing and different way to serve zucchini – simple too! Use different herbs if you wish.

Serves 4

INGREDIENTS:

4 large zucchini

1 cup sundried tomatoes

2 cloves garlic

1 cup chopped fresh tomatoes

1 cup water

¼ cucumber, grated

3 tablespoons hemp oil

1 tablespoon balsamic vinegar

¾ teaspoon each oregano, thyme and rosemary (fresh)

Sea salt to taste

DIRECTIONS:

1. Soak the sundried tomatoes in water for 20 minutes.
2. Meanwhile, shave the zucchini with a vegetable peeler to make thin, strip noodles.
3. Place the sundried tomatoes, when soaked, in a food processor, together with all of the other ingredients except the 'pasta'.
4. Process until smooth.
5. Mix into the zucchini and serve.

Nutritional Facts per Serving: *Calories 196, Fat 11.7g, Carbs 21.7g, Dietary Fiber 6.3g, Protein 6.5g*

101 Flavorful Plant-Based Recipes For Athletic Performance

CAULIFLOWER SALAD

A tender cauliflower salad with a healthy twist! Add chopped red bell pepper and chili for extra color and a zing.

Serves 4

INGREDIENTS:

1 head cauliflower, broken into florets

2 stalks celery, diced

4 tablespoons finely chopped red onion

1 tablespoon finely chopped parsley

2 tablespoons olive oil

1 tablespoon Dijon mustard

½ teaspoon sea salt

DIRECTIONS:

1. Steam the cauliflower until just tender. Allow to cool and then place in a large bowl.
2. Add the celery, onion and parsley.
3. Whisk together the olive oil, mustard and salt.
4. Pour over the cauliflower.
5. Leave in the fridge for an hour or so for the flavors to develop.
6. Serve.

Nutritional Facts per Serving: *Calories 87, Fat 7.3g, Carbs 5.4g, Dietary Fiber 2.4g, Protein 1.9g*

Vegan Athlete Cookbook

SUMMER SALAD WITH POPPY SEED DRESSING

Any salad with poppy seed dressing is scrumptious! This is no exception! Eat straight away as the salad does not keep.

Serves 4

INGREDIENTS:

8 cups baby spinach

2 cups red seedless grapes, halved

2 cups chopped sweet red onion

2 cups chopped tofu

¾ cup golden raisins

½ cup slivered almonds

1/3 cup olive oil

¼ cup Vegan sugar

3 tablespoons balsamic vinegar

2 tablespoons sesame seeds

1 tablespoon poppy seeds

1 finely chopped small shallot

¼ teaspoon paprika

¼ teaspoon Worcestershire sauce (Vegan)

DIRECTIONS:

1. Make the dressing by whizzing in a blender the oil, sugar, vinegar, seeds, shallot, paprika and Worcestershire sauce.
2. Combine the other ingredients in a large bowl. Mix.
3. Serve the salad tossed in the poppy seed dressing.

Nutritional Facts per Serving: *Calories 557, Fat 31.6g, Carbs 61.3g, Dietary Fiber 7.5g, Protein 17.7g*

101 Flavorful Plant-Based Recipes For Athletic Performance

SUMMER FRUITS WITH CHICKPEAS

An energy boosting salad for a pre-workout meal! The strawberry sauce is outstanding.

Serves 4

INGREDIENTS:

2 cups cooked and drained chickpeas

2 cups cantaloupe melon, cubed

1 cup fresh blueberries

1 cup diced celery

4 cups fresh raw baby spinach

½ cup toasted slivered almonds

1/3 cup organic agave nectar

1/3 cup rice vinegar

8 medium strawberries, hulled

Salt and pepper to taste

Extra strawberries for serving

DIRECTIONS:

1. Combine the chickpeas, melon, blueberries and celery in a large bowl.
2. Make the strawberry dressing by whizzing the agave nectar, vinegar and hulled strawberries in a blender.
3. Pour the dressing over the pea and fruit mix. Season to taste.
4. Place a cup of spinach on each of 4 plates. Top with the salad and garnish with the toasted almonds and some extra strawberries.

Nutritional Facts per Serving: *Calories 612, Fat 12.4g, Carbs 104.2g, Dietary Fiber 22.7g, Protein 24.4g*

STUFFED ACORN SQUASH

Serve on its own or with burger patties for an extra filling meal.

Serves 4

INGREDIENTS:

1 acorn squash

3 cups chopped celery

1 cup chopped onion

½ chopped red bell pepper

2 cups apple sauce

Teaspoon mild curry powder

1 teaspoon cinnamon

1 tablespoon vegetable seasoning

14 ounces baby spinach

Salt and pepper to taste

DIRECTIONS:

1. Pre-heat the oven to 350°F. Place ¼ inch of water in the bottom of a baking tray.
2. Halve the squash and place cut side down on the baking sheet. Bake for 45 minutes until tender.
3. Stir together the apple sauce, curry, cinnamon and vegetable seasoning.
4. Turn the squash over when cooked and fill with the apple mixture. Bake for a further 10 minutes.
5. Steam the spinach until wilted. Serve the squash on a bed of spinach. Check the seasoning.

Nutritional Facts per Serving: *Calories 131, Fat 1.1g, Carbs 28.2g, Dietary Fiber 7.1g, Protein 5.0g*

101 Flavorful Plant-Based Recipes For Athletic Performance

CURRIED SWEET POTATOES

These potatoes have a Thai flavor intertwined! Enjoy. This could be classed as a main meal as it contains a generous serving of tofu.

Serves 4

INGREDIENTS:

1 cup uncooked brown basmati rice

1 pound sweet potatoes, cubed

1 x 15 ounce can coconut milk

3 teaspoons Thai red curry paste

½ cup chopped cilantro

1 x 14 ounce packet firm tofu, drained and cubed

1 tablespoon peanut oil

3 tablespoons soy sauce

5 thinly sliced shallots

4 baby bok choy

1 fresh lime

DIRECTIONS:

1. Rinse the rice and cook in plenty of salt water until tender.
2. Heat the coconut milk and water together in a skillet over a medium high heat.
3. Stir in the curry paste, cilantro and sweet potatoes. Lower the heat.
4. In another skillet toast the tofu and add the peanut oil, salt and soy sauce. Make sure it is not too salty.
5. Cook together for about 3 minutes and then add to the sweet potatoes.

Vegan Athlete Cookbook

6. Whip out the tofu skillet and add a little more peanut oil. Add the shallots and caramelize, 4 to 5 minutes.

7. In a small saucepan, simmer the bok choy in some salted water until tender but still with a bite.

8. Put the rice on a plate and top with the sweet potato mixture. Serve the bok choy on the side.

9. Garnish with the shallots and wedges of lime.

Nutritional Facts per Serving: *Calories 675, Fat 34.6g, Carbs 79.0g, Dietary Fiber 9.1g, Protein 17.1g*

101 Flavorful Plant-Based Recipes For Athletic Performance

SAUCES & DIPS

TAHINI-MISO SAUCE

A traditional sauce. Add some crushed garlic for a different flavor. This sauce will keep for a week in the fridge. Add a little more water if it becomes too thick with keeping.

Serves 4

INGREDIENTS:

1 tablespoon Tahini

2 teaspoons red miso

2 teaspoons fresh lime juice

1 tablespoon vegetable stock

DIRECTIONS:

1. Mix all of the ingredients to the required consistency.
2. Add water if you wish for a thinner sauce.
3. Serve over crisp vegetables, wilted greens or pasta.
4. Line a loaf shaped baking tin with parchment paper which has been greased with a little coconut oil.

Nutritional Facts per Serving: *Calories 30, Fat 2.2g, Carbs 2.1g, Dietary Fiber 0.7g, Protein 1.0g*

101 Flavorful Plant-Based Recipes For Athletic Performance

BARBEQUE SAUCE

A smooth or chunky sauce to serve with a barbeque, or over pasta!

Serves 16

INGREDIENTS:

1 tablespoon vegetable oil

1 medium sized onion, minced

4 cloves garlic, minced

¼ teaspoon salt

1 teaspoon dried chili flakes

2 x 15 ounce cans chopped tomatoes

¼ cup molasses

¼ cup white vinegar

2 tablespoons brown sugar

1 tablespoon prepared mustard

2 teaspoons liquid smoke

DIRECTIONS:

1. Sauté the onion in the oil until brown. Add the garlic and cook for another minute.
2. Add all of the other ingredients except the mustard and liquid smoke. Cook for 45 minutes, uncovered, over a low heat, stirring occasionally.
3. Add the mustard and liquid smoke. Stir and taste test.
4. Adjust as you think necessary, cooking for 5 more minutes.
5. Whizz in a blender if you wish for a smooth sauce. Serve.

Nutritional Facts per Serving: *Calories 42, Fat 1.0g, Carbs 8.0g, Dietary Fiber 0.8g, Protein 0.6g*

BABA GHANOUSH

A Middle Eastern dip or spread similar to hummus, but made with eggplant! Enjoy with veggies, pita or as a filling for a wrap and add some chopped fresh chili if you dare.

Serves 8

INGREDIENTS:

1 large eggplant

1 can chickpeas, washed and drained

4 cloves garlic, crushed

½ cup fresh lemon juice

3 tablespoons tahina paste

Pinch of sea salt

¼ cup olive oil

2 tablespoons chopped parsley

DIRECTIONS:

1. Pre-heat the oven to 400°F.
2. Slice the eggplant in half and roast in the hot oven for about 45 minutes until soft.
3. Remove the eggplant from the oven and cool.
4. Scoop out the flesh and place it in a blender with the other ingredients except the oil and the parsley.
5. Blend until smooth. Gradually blend in the oil until well mixed.
6. Spoon into a serving bowl and sprinkle with chopped parsley.

Nutritional Facts per Serving: *Calories 318, Fat 14.3g, Carbs 37.2g, Dietary Fiber 11.8g, Protein 12.6g*

101 Flavorful Plant-Based Recipes For Athletic Performance

CREAMY SPINACH AND ARTICHOKE DIP

This dip is best served warm as a dunk for cucumber and bell pepper slices! Also good with corn chips or whole wheat biscuits.

Serves: 12

INGREDIENTS:

20 ounces frozen, chopped spinach

2 x 14 ounce jars artichoke hearts

1 tablespoon olive oil

1 cup diced red onion

3 cloves garlic, minced

Salt to taste

1 teaspoon onion powder

½ teaspoon each of garlic powder, black pepper, cayenne pepper

1 tablespoon fresh lemon juice

1½ cups cashew cream

DIRECTIONS:

1. Defrost the spinach and squeeze out the excess water. Set aside.
2. Drain and chop the artichokes.
3. Sauté the onions in the oil until translucent, about 10 minutes. Add the garlic and cook for another minute.
4. Stir in the artichokes and all of the seasonings and heat through. Add the spinach, lemon juice and heat again.
5. Stir in the cashew cream

Nutritional Facts per Serving: *Calories 112, Fat 5.4g, Carbs 14.2g, Dietary Fiber 5.1g, Protein 5.0g*

Vegan Athlete Cookbook

SWEET CHILI SAUCE

A sauce to top all else – well at least your veggies! This sauce will keep in a screw topped jar in the fridge for about 3 weeks. But, will it last that long? Doubt it!

Serves 8

INGREDIENTS:

½ cup chopped and seeded red bell pepper

4 tablespoons agave nectar

2 heaped tablespoons soaked and minced sun dried tomatoes

2 teaspoons onion powder

1 teaspoon minced garlic

1 teaspoon fresh ginger, finely grated

1 teaspoon dried chili flakes

4 tablespoons fresh lime juice

1/3 cup apple cider vinegar

½ cup water

½ teaspoon sea salt

DIRECTIONS:

1. Place all of the ingredients into a blender.
2. Blend.
3. Serve.

Nutritional Facts per Serving: *Calories 39, Fat 0.8g, Carbs 8.0g, Dietary Fiber 0.9g, Protein 0.4g*

POWER PACKED PUDDINGS & COOKIES

Vegan Athlete Cookbook

CHOCOLATE ZUCCHINI CUPCAKES

Moist and delicious with a nutty flavor and texture! Try apples, beets or carrots instead of the zucchini. Increase the sugar by a couple of tablespoons if you like a sweeter muffin. Coconut milk could be used too.

Makes 12

INGREDIENTS:

1½ cups whole wheat pastry flour

¼ cup unsweetened cocoa powder

¾ cup brown superfine sugar

1 teaspoon baking powder

½ teaspoon salt

1 cup rice milk

1 tablespoon apple cider vinegar

2 tablespoons coconut oil

2 tablespoons unsweetened apple sauce

1 teaspoon vanilla extract

1 cup shredded zucchini

DIRECTIONS:

1. Pre-heat the oven to 350°F.
2. Line a 12 cup muffin tin with paper liners.
3. Combine the milk and the vinegar in a jug. Let stand until it curdles.
4. In a large bowl mix together all of the dry ingredients and make a well in the centre.
5. Add the curdled milk, oil, apple sauce and vanilla and stir until just combined. Stir in the zucchini.
6. Divide the batter between the 12 muffin cups.

101 Flavorful Plant-Based Recipes For Athletic Performance

7. Bake for 15 - 20 minutes until cooked through.
8. Remove the muffins from the oven and cool in the tin for 5 minutes before moving to a rack to cool completely.

Nutritional Facts per Serving: *Calories 138, Fat 3.0g, Carbs 26.9g, Dietary Fiber 2.2g, Protein 2.0g*

Vegan Athlete Cookbook

COOKIES A LA VEGAN!

Lemon and vanilla combine in these super, crispy, crunchy and munchy cookies.

Makes 20

INGREDIENTS:

1½ cups palm oil shortening

2/3 cup brown superfine sugar

1 teaspoon vanilla extract

1½ tablespoons fresh lemon juice

3 cups all-purpose flour mixed with ½ teaspoon baking powder

1 teaspoon salt

DIRECTIONS:

1. Pre-heat the oven to 325°F.
2. Line 2 cookie sheets with parchment paper and oil lightly with some coconut oil.
3. Mix together the flour, salt and baking powder.
4. Beat the palm oil shortening with the sugar until fluffy. Add the vanilla and the lemon juice.
5. Stir in the dry ingredients, making sure everything comes together. If necessary add a little more lemon juice.
6. Wrap the dough in plastic wrap and chill for about an hour.
7. Roll the dough into a cylinder shape. Cut 20 x ¼ inch slices and place these on the cookie sheet.
8. Bake for 20 – 25 minutes until starting to turn brown.
9. Cool and serve.

Nutritional Facts per Serving: *Calories 238, Fat 15.6g, Carbs 22.9g, Dietary Fiber 0.5g, Protein 1.9g*

101 Flavorful Plant-Based Recipes For Athletic Performance

FRUITY CHOCOLATE CHIP SCONES

Tiny triangular scones brimming full of energy and flavor! Ice them if you wish by making an icing with powdered sugar, vanilla extract and some water, mixed to a thin paste and lightly drizzled over the treat.

Makes 32 small scones

INGREDIENTS:

2 cups cooked lentils

2 tablespoons ground flaxseed

¼ cup warm water

2¼ cups all-purpose flour

½ cup rolled oats

1 tablespoon baking powder

1 teaspoon salt

½ teaspoon cinnamon

½ cup dark chocolate chips

½ cup pitted Medjool dates

6 tablespoons agave nectar

1 teaspoon almond extract

DIRECTIONS:

1. Pre-heat the oven to 400°F.
2. Line a cookie sheet with parchment paper.
3. In a small bowl mix the flaxseeds with the warm water and set aside to thicken.
4. In a large bowl stir together the flour, oats, baking powder, salt, cinnamon and chocolate chips.
5. In a food processor, process the lentils, dates. Agave nectar, almond extract and flaxseed paste until smooth.

6. Fold the lentil mixture into the dry ingredients. Combine well.

7. Turn the mixture out onto a floured board and flatten with your hands into a 10 x 10 inch square, about ½ inch thick.

8. Cut the dough into 16 equal squares. Cut each square in half diagonally.

9. Place the triangles onto the baking sheet about an inch apart.

10. Bake for 15 minutes until puffed up and firm.

11. Remove from the oven and cool on a wire rack.

Nutritional Facts per Serving: *Calories 111, Fat 0.9g, Carbs 21.4g, Dietary Fiber 4.6g, Protein 4.5g*

101 Flavorful Plant-Based Recipes For Athletic Performance

CORN AND CHIA WAFFLES

You will need a waffle iron to make these! Top with fresh fruit or maple syrup. Or why not both?

Makes 5

INGREDIENTS:

¼ cup finely ground corn meal

¼ cup chia seeds

¼ cup oats, ground

½ teaspoon salt

1 teaspoon baking powder

½ cup apple sauce

1 cup hemp milk

1 tablespoon coconut oil

1 tablespoon maple syrup

1 teaspoon vanilla extract

DIRECTIONS:

1. Stir together the corn meal, chia, oats, salt and baking powder.
2. In a separate bowl mix all of the other ingredients. The coconut oil may need to be warmed slightly.
3. Stir the wet ingredients into the dry and combine to a smooth batter.
4. Spray the waffle iron with non-stick spray and pour in the batter.
5. Follow the directions for your waffle iron and remove each waffle as it cooks. Serve hot!

Nutritional Facts per Serving: *Calories 123, Fat 6.3g, Carbs 16.5g, Dietary Fiber 3.2g, Protein 2.4g*

PINEAPPLE UPSIDE DOWN CAKE

Here's a traditional favorite for Vegans! This is a delicious cake which can be served for tea or as a dessert.

Serves 10

INGREDIENTS:

1½ cups flour

1 cup sugar

1 teaspoon baking soda

½ teaspoon salt

¾ cup pineapple juice from the canned pineapple

¼ cup water

¼ cup apple sauce

1 tablespoon lemon juice

1 20 ounce can pineapple chunks in unsweetened syrup

¼ cup loosely packed brown sugar

DIRECTIONS:

1. Pre-heat the oven to 350°F.
2. Prepare a 12 inch spring-form baking tin.
3. Mix flour, sugar, baking soda and salt in a large bowl.
4. Drain the pineapple, reserving ¾ cup juice. Add water to make 1 cup.
5. In a separate bowl combine the apple sauce, lemon juice and the pineapple water.
6. Place the pineapple chunks on the base of the baking tin. Sprinkle with the brown sugar.
7. Mix together the dry and the wet ingredients and pour over the pineapple and sugar.

8. Place in the oven and bake for 25 – 30 minutes until firm and cooked through.
9. Remove the cake from the oven and let it cool. Loosen the sides of the cake tin and turn out onto a serving plate, pineapple side up!

Nutritional Facts per Serving: *Calories 197, Fat 0.3g, Carbs 47.3g, Dietary Fiber 1.0g, Protein 2.4g*

Vegan Athlete Cookbook

DATE AND BLUEBERRY MUFFINS

Moist, gooey muffins – sensational! The smells coming from the kitchen when these are cooking are superb!

Makes 12

INGREDIENTS:

2 tablespoons flax meal

6 tablespoons water

1 cup almond flour

1 cup coconut flour

2 teaspoons baking soda

1 teaspoon sea salt

2 tablespoons mixed spice

1 cup dates, pitted

2 cups canned pumpkin

1 teaspoon lemon juice

¼ cup coconut oil

5 ounces frozen blueberries

¾ cup zucchini, grated

¾ cup chopped walnuts

DIRECTIONS:

1. Preheat oven to 350° F.
2. Line 12 muffin cups with paper liners.
3. Mix together the flax meal and water and leave for a few minutes until it becomes a gel-like consistency.
4. Mix almond flour, coconut flour, baking soda, sea salt and mixed spice in large bowl. Set aside.

101 Flavorful Plant-Based Recipes For Athletic Performance

5. In a food processor, pulse together the pitted dates, pumpkin and lemon juice together with the flax water and coconut oil.

6. Mix the pumpkin mixture into the dry ingredients. Mix well.

7. Gently stir in the blueberries, grated zucchini and walnuts.

8. Divide the mixture evenly between the prepared muffin cups.

9. Bake for about 30 minutes. If the muffins are too gooey, after this time, leave for a few minutes longer.

Nutritional Facts per Serving: *Calories 211, Fat 12.0g, Carbs 23.3g, Dietary Fiber 7.2g, Protein 5.0g*

CRANBERRY AND LEMON COOKIES

Cranberries, nuts, apple and lemon combine in these excellent lunch box fillers. These will keep for a few days in an airtight container – that is if there are any left!

Makes 12

INGREDIENTS:

½ cup coconut milk

1 tablespoon ground flaxseed

1¼ cups brown organic superfine sugar

½ cup unsweetened apple sauce

¼ cup vegetable oil

1 tablespoon fresh lemon juice

1½ teaspoons lemon zest

2 teaspoons vanilla extract

1¼ cups unbleached general purpose flour

1 cup whole wheat flour

1 teaspoon baking soda

½ teaspoon salt

1 cup dried cranberries

1 cup chopped walnuts

DIRECTIONS:

1. Pre-heat the oven to 350°F.
2. Prepare 2 cookie sheets with parchment paper.
3. Warm the coconut milk and stir in the flaxseed. Leave to one side for it to gel.
4. In a large bowl, stir together all of the wet ingredients with the

sugar. Stir in the gelled flax seed.

5. In another bowl sift together the flours, baking soda and salt.

6. Add the flour mix to the wet ingredients a little at a time until fully combined.

7. When a dough has formed stir in the nuts and cranberries.

8. Using a spoon form 2 inch round cookies on the prepared sheets.

9. Bake for 12 – 15 minutes until a nice golden brown.

10. Remove from the oven and leave to rest on the cookie sheet for about 5 minutes. Place on a cooling rack.

11. Serve, eat and enjoy!

Nutritional Facts per Serving: *Calories 332, Fat 13.6g, Carbs 48.8g, Dietary Fiber 2.4g, Protein 4.9g*

Vegan Athlete Cookbook

NO BAKE OAT COOKIES

Fast, fantastic and filling! Also popular with children, and simple enough for them to join you in the kitchen to help make them.

Makes 24

INGREDIENTS:

½ cup plain soy milk

1¾ cups sugar

½ cup Vegan butter

1 teaspoon vanilla extract

3½ cups quick cooking oats

¼ cup unsweetened cocoa powder

½ cup smooth or crunchy peanut butter

DIRECTIONS:

1. In a small pot combine the milk, butter, sugar, peanut butter and vanilla and cook until smooth and creamy
2. In a large bowl combine the oats and cocoa powder.
3. Pour the warm milk mixture over the oats and stir until all the ingredients have combined.
4. Place dollops of mixture onto a waxed paper lined cookie sheet and let cool for about half an hour.

Nutritional Facts per Serving: *Calories 171, Fat 6.7g, Carbs 25.5g, Dietary Fiber 2.0g, Protein 3.3g*

101 Flavorful Plant-Based Recipes For Athletic Performance

THANK YOU

If you enjoyed this, and I'm guessing your taste buds did, please check out some of the other recipe books I've created, available at Amazon.

Thanks so much to my family, and friends, and to all those pursuing healthy active living within the Vegan community.

Be good to each other!

Zoey Sampson

Printed in Poland
by Amazon Fulfillment
Poland Sp. z o.o., Wrocław